FRONTIER Texas!

A Journey through the Wild West

FRONTIER Texas!

A Journey through the Wild West

Abilene Christian University Press

Cover illustration by H. C. Zachry

FRONTIER *Texas!*

A Journey through the Wild West

ISBN 978-0-89112-592-1

Material for this book was primarily taken from the information presented in the exhibits at Frontier Texas! The arrangement and editing of the information and supplemental content was provided by Kim Snyder, Jeff Salmon, and H. C. Zachry. Content direction and suggestions were graciously provided by Donald Frazier, PhD and Pyramid Studios. The photography for the exhibits was provided by Chris Allen, Rebecca Kinnison, and Jeff Salmon of the Frontier Texas! staff. Other photography, illustrations, and artifact ownership is credited throughout the volume as the images appear.

Printed in Canada

Cover and interior design by Becky Hawley Design

For information contact:
Abilene Christian University Press
1626 Campus Court
Abilene, Texas 79601

1-877-816-4455 toll free
www.acupressbooks.com

Table of Contents

"IF THE CATTLE STARTED RUNNING YOU'D HEAR
THAT LOW RUMBLING NOISE. THEN YOU'D JUMP
ON YOUR HORSE–RIDING AT A DEAD RUN IN THE
DARK–NOT KNOWING IF THE NEXT JUMP WOULD
LAND YOU IN A SHALLOW GRAVE."
–Cowboy Edward C. "Teddy Blue" Abbott
DANGERS OF THE TRAIL
Stampedes, Indians, outlaws, and severe weather were a constant threat on the trail.

Preface

This book will provide you with a factual basis for the romance of the wild west in Texas, specifically in the region bordered by the Red River on the north, Interstate 10 on the south, Fort Worth on the east and the Caprock of the Great Plains on the west. That is the region we call frontier Texas, because so many of the individuals and stories of the old west were tied to this area.

In telling this hugely important story, the book will also reveal how the Frontier Texas! facility, in which the story is presented, came to be.

Frontier Texas! can, in a way, be traced back to the 1981 Abilene Centennial Celebration. As chair of the Centennial Celebration, I was seeking to dispose of some remaining funds, hopefully on a permanent improvement project. The most obvious need for downtown visual improvement was the railroad right of way.

The railroad right of way had scratched an ugly path through the center of town for 100 years, just a stretch of rocks, prickly pear and trash. I began to work with railroad officials and though reluctant because of the lack of precedents, they eventually leased the right of way to the City of Abilene to landscape.

Under the guidance of Joe Canon, Dodge Jones Foundation (in their first major project for downtown Abilene) funded the purchase of 600 trees and irrigation equipment, with the City staff installing. First plantings were in 1982, with more trees added annually until the entire path was landscaped. Bless Judy Matthews and Dodge Jones Foundation, as they went on to fund the Paramount Theatre restoration in 1986 and the Grace Museum in 1989 and with these three projects, launched the revitalization of downtown that continues today.

FACING PAGE: *The* Cowboys and Longhorns *area of Frontier Texas! takes you on an early cattle drive.*

ABOVE: *A full-size tipi contains many rare artifacts, such as this buffalo hide berry pounding bowl and stone pounder.*

One goal of Frontier Texas! was the visual improvement of downtown Abilene. This was accomplished as the existing junk yard site was converted into a regional cultural/educational facility.

The City staff was finally able to purchase from the railroad the land being used as a switching yard and metal recycling business at North 2nd and Treadaway and to relocate the metal recycling center. There were no plans for the area—just a general hope that the visual blight could be removed.

As an idea, I approached T. D. Kelsey, a sculptor with an international reputation about doing a 75-foot long sculpture of cowboys and longhorns for the available site. He produced a 3-foot clay macquette of the proposed sculpture, which I hauled around Abilene for a year or so to generate interest. Then, Dallas announced a similar project (and had the money to do it). Their preemption deflated me. Our plan was dropped, because I thought Abilene should be unique, not “me too.”

Not long after, the Texas legislature announced the new availability of matching state funds to help build visitor centers. Hearing that, I developed a concept that included both a visitor center and a cultural-historical ‘experience” based on the early “wild west” history of our region of Texas.

The story was confined to the 1780 to 1880 period—just 100 years which contained so much conflict, cultural devastation, empires rising and falling, industries being created and destroyed, peoples conquering and being conquered—so much simultaneous misery and happiness—and all mostly shoehorned into just a century. Limiting the facility to this period served two purposes: it collected and presented the fragmented story of this area of Texas into a concise presentation, and it respected our budget—we didn't have the money to tell a story from the beginning of time to the current day.

So, our story starts in a raw, wild bloody wilderness in the 1700s and ends with the railroad crossing the region and bringing civilization—or, at least, that moment's version of civilization, in 1881.

Abilene is in a region where much of the frontier history of Texas occurred. Experiences of Indians, cowboys, outlaws, soldiers, buffalo hunters, and settlers stimulated hundreds of books and movies that made Texas known around the world, but our region's part of those adventures had never been collected into an overall regional story. Frontier Texas! would visualize that experience in a unique presentation unlike any other historical facility anywhere, giving Abilene a cultural-historical facility that was one-of-a-kind.

The typical museum approach to a historical story is to show artifacts and describe how they relate to the times. Problem was, we had very few artifacts. So, instead, we resolved to use the latest technology to "bring people back to life." Selected individuals, long dead, but who were an integral part of our western story, were re-created with the wonders of technology. They appear as real as when, two centuries ago, they struggled, suffered, rejoiced, lost, won, lived or died—and they tell you about what it was like to experience those defeats and victories.

We have a few artifacts—but that is hardly the word for them. They are world-class, one-of-a-kind personal items of the people who were deeply involved in our region's story. You can only see them at Frontier Texas!

The Owen Foundation provided the initial major underwriting for the endeavor, with Dian Owen leading them into their largest project to date. Tucker Bridwell, her CEO, spearheaded the scramble (more like a battle) in Austin for a portion of the State funds. Dodge Jones Foundation immediately made a very significant commitment to the project. Many, many companies and individuals provided financial help, though it was somewhat murky what the final product would be.

Recognizing that non-profit facilities are never self-sustaining, the organizers of Frontier Texas! and the City coordinated a public election to increase the Venue Tax (a hotel occupancy tax) to help subsidize operating revenues (Nancy Liles of the ACVB had the initial idea). Later, the Abilene ISD's Shotwell Stadium and the Taylor County Expo Center were designated to receive part of the proposed venue tax increase.

This original business plan has worked for Frontier Texas! as the facility operates "in the black" with a portion of the venue tax funds, gate admissions and gift shop sales. Periodically, exhibit revisions are made through the donations of generous individuals and entities.

After three years, 10,000 square feet and almost $12 million dollars, the debt-free facility opened. Thousands of people from all over the world have now visited Frontier Texas!, leaving with an improved appreciation of our region's role in one of the most volatile and exciting segments of America's entire history. Recently, a "refreshing" of the story provided an opportunity to add more historical context, so a segment on very early Texas (15,000 years ago) was added.

There's a chapter in this book, "The Making of Frontier Texas!" that will give you more detail about the who/what of the facility's creation, but I thought you might enjoy knowing a bit about its early genetics.

This book is published to meet a need. Thousands of people from across the globe have asked for a printed copy of the story told in Frontier Texas! They want to be able to relive the experience they have just seen. As well, the staff so often hears from visitors, "I wish you had a book that I could give to. . . ."

So, here it is. The book is not like being immersed in the actual experience of Frontier Texas! You must come here for that. But, regardless, you are going to enjoy seeing the story unfold through these pages in your hands.

H. C. Zachry
Concept Originator of Frontier Texas!

The buffalo bone pile at Frontier Texas! on the very spot on which similar bones were piled for rail shipment in the late 1800s. A boneyard was the first commercial use of this site.

Blood and Treasure on the Frontier

Frontier Texas! in Abilene and this book are here to help guide you on a trail of history, actually the crossroads of a lot of historical trails. If you like adventure, you've come to the right place.

In just a few decades this region of Texas was transformed from an open prairie—the stomping grounds of Indians and cowboys, and buffalo hunters, outlaws and cavalry—into the ranchlands and hometowns of pioneer Texans.

"A great country for men and dogs, but hell on women and horses."

—old Texas proverb

People all over the world know about Texas, mostly from the thousands of movies and books about the Wild West and adventures on the frontier. Many of these stories and adventures took place is this section of Texas, bordered by the Red River on the north, San Antonio on the south, the Caprock on the west and Fort Worth on the east. This area was the wild frontier.

Think of the frontier as a line between the known and the unknown. It was never like a line on a map. It was more like the line that separates people of different cultures, different languages, and different ideas about what is valuable.

The story of Frontier Texas! is a story about blood and treasure—different people looking for whatever was their own treasure. And, a lot of blood was spilled in the fight to see whose ideas and whose ways would win out.

The first native people in this area lived here about fifteen thousand years ago. The following centuries saw different groups come and go. Some were starved out by nature; some moved on, likely to find an easier place to make it; some were run out or destroyed by other invading tribes. This is a hard land. It never gave in easy to people's ideas of success, and sometimes it doesn't even give in to survival.

Four or five hundred years ago, the main people here were called the Jumano. They were kin to the Anasazi Indians out in Pueblo country. The Jumano were pushed out by the Apaches.

About two hundred years later, something huge happened that changed everything—the Comanche Indians, living then in the foothills of the Rocky Mountains, traded for horses from the Pueblo Indians. The Pueblo, in what is now New Mexico, revolted from domination by the Spanish, killing most of them and driving the rest back to El Paso—leaving behind the Spanish horses. The Comanche traded for horses and, in no time, began to ride, hunt and raid like no force the country had seen before. The Comanche pushed the Apaches out of Texas and New Mexico, and, within just fifty years or so, became totally dominant in this huge region. They were to rule this area, in war and peace, for nearly two centuries.

That sets the stage for the real beginning of this story. And as you read through this adventure, you're going to meet some amazing people. You'll stand at that line that divided the whites and the Indians. Sometimes that line even divided the Indians . . . as well as the whites. You'll meet some people who crossed the line, both ways, and didn't want to come back.

Settlers, possessing the European view of land ownership, saw this country as empty and free for the taking by anyone with guts and gumption. The Comanche were nomadic, but as long as territory was in their "range," they considered it theirs. It was a time of bloody conflict—a time when both whites and Indians were murdered and scalped, in a land where law did not exist.

While a few early settlers began coming in, this was still a wide-open land, even after the buffalo began being killed off. The pursuit of the buffalo and their eventual absence opened up a whole new kind of opportunity for pioneers who would risk getting scalped—an opportunity that involved cattle. Wild longhorns. They offered livelihood and sometimes wealth for many displaced southerners following the Civil War as they developed trail drives to get longhorns from the open range to railroads and markets in states to the north.

With all the mix of buffalo hunters, cowboys, soldiers, and settlers, little ramshackle camps and settlements started sprouting up around the forts and the main trail crossings. They were wild places—saloons, gambling dens, you name it. In and around them were good people, bad people, and some who seemed to move back and forth.

The Butterfield Overland Stage, the longest wheeled trip in the world, passed right through this area. Between St. Louis and San Francisco, the Stage covered 2790 miles, stopping every twenty miles to change horses. It passed through frontier Texas with stops at Fort Belknap, Fort Phantom Hill, Castle Peak and on down to Fort Chadbourne and Fort Concho. But, it was just too expensive to operate and at the start of the Civil War, the Butterfield came to an end and never started up again.

The people of frontier Texas could not foresee the changes ahead, but still they came, traveling from far away to build their homes, laying down their lives when necessary—each generation sacrificing so the next could survive and prosper.

The wild west was truly wild in many situations. But when it got a foothold, civilization came on fast. It rode in on the railroad in 1880 and 81. In fact, that's how Abilene got its start, as a railroad town.

Just as the buffalo and wild horses had given way to fences and cattle, and the Indians to waves of settlers, the uncertainty of our frontier began to give way to a completely different world where there would be much to learn, to understand . . . and to accept.

So, how can this amazing rough and tumble story be told? We think it is best related through the people—men and women, young and old—who, long ago, left their homes in civilized lands to start anew in a faraway place called Texas.

Through those people, real people who were a part of it, you will learn about the frontier—the wild west—for which Texas is known around the world.

Buck Taylor, a star of the television show Gunsmoke *and actor in dozens of movies, is the Trail Guide for visitors to Frontier Texas!*

Texas History Timeline

Small Bands of Indigenous Peoples Roam Across Texas

4000
Atlatl replaces thrusting spear

700
Bow and arrow replaces the atlatl

1541
Coronado explores Texas region

1600
Apache Indians displace the Jumano

1691
El Camino Real, —oldest U.S. highway established

1700
Comanche claim the region as home

1716–89
Spain establishes Catholic missions in Texas

1724
Apache displaced by the Comanche

1759
Comanches destroy Mission Santa Cruz de San Saba

Comancheria

10,000 BC | 5,000 BC | 0 | 1000 | 1500 | 1550 | 1600 | 1650 | 1700 | 1720 | 1740 | 1760 | 1780

Outside Texas

1492
Columbus sails to the Americas

1607
Colonists arrive at Jamestown

1776
U.S. Declaration of Independence signed

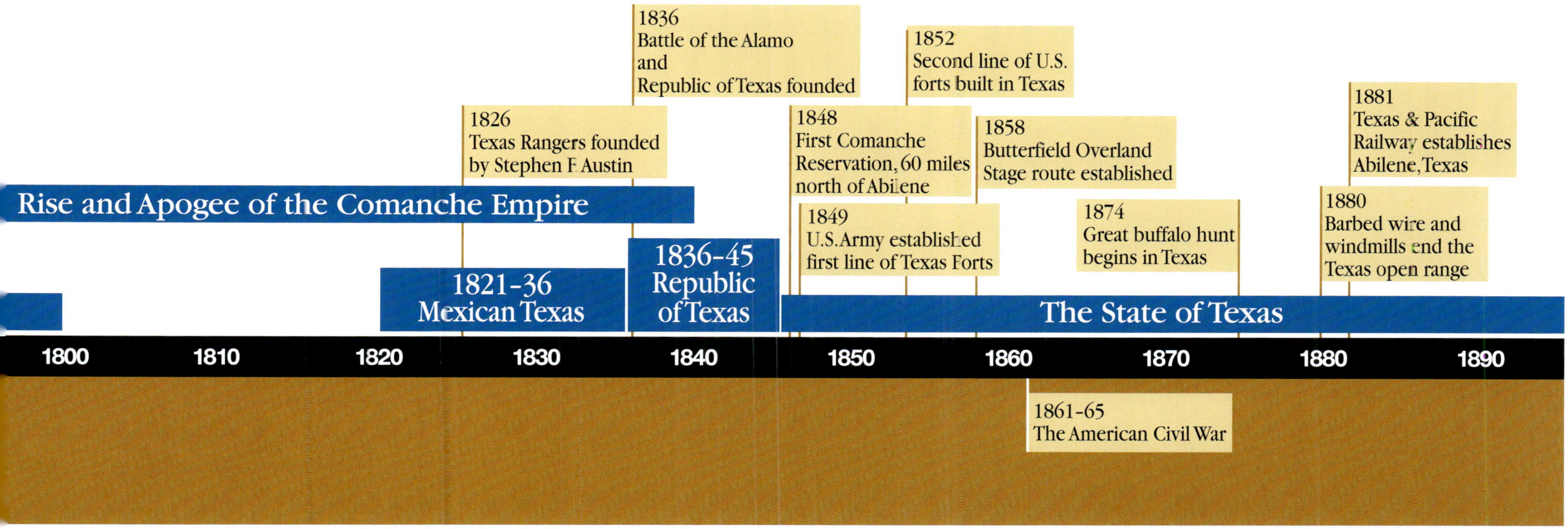

1836
Battle of the Alamo
and
Republic of Texas founded
1852
Second line of U.S.
forts built in Texas
1881
Texas & Pacific
Railway establishes
Abilene, Texas
1826
Texas Rangers founded
by Stephen F. Austin
1848
First Comanche
Reservation, 60 miles
north of Abilene
1858
Butterfield Overland
Stage route established
Rise and Apogee of the Comanche Empire
1849
U.S. Army established
first line of Texas Forts
1874
Great buffalo hunt
begins in Texas
1880
Barbed wire and
windmills end the
Texas open range
1821-36
Mexican Texas
1836-45
Republic
of Texas
The State of Texas
1800
1810
1820
1830
1840
1850
1860
1870
1880
1890
1861-65
The American Civil War

The Sequence of the Frontier Texas! Experiences

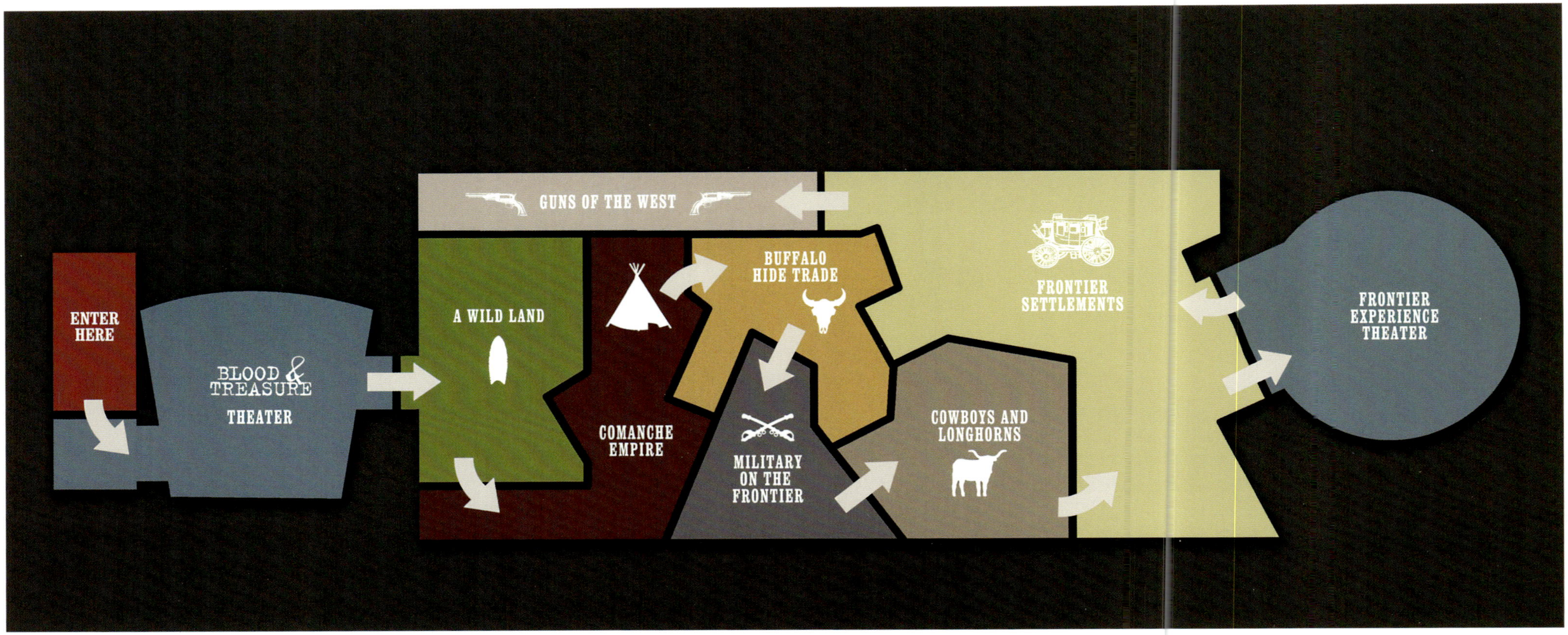

A Wild Land

Cultures have struggled with the forces of this region for 15,000 years.

CHAPTER 1

For almost 15,000 years before the Texas frontier was settled, humans traveled through this region on foot.

But this was no place to make a permanent home. It was a harsh land, and each day was a life or death struggle.

Climate alternated between ice ages, and torrid heat and drought cycles. One culture after another disappeared from the ravages of weather, wild animals or human enemies.

But around 1700, the Comanche—riding horses introduced to the New World by Spanish explorers—claimed this region as home.

This wild and perilous land was about to get a lot wilder, and a lot more dangerous.

The First Humans

It's believed that humans first entered America across Alaska's Bering Strait between 15,000 and 25,000 years ago.

The first evidence of early habitation in America, the Clovis Man, was found 150 miles west of Abilene near Clovis, New Mexico. These Paleo Indians hunted ice-age mammoths and giant bison with thrusting spears.

Extreme climate changes may have caused the extinction of the large animals—and Clovis Man.

Folsom Man is likely a descendant of Clovis Man. Severe heat may have ended the Folsom culture.

A 300-year drought followed, ruining crops and initiating migration and conflict. As a result, the Anasazi, ancestors of the Pueblos, created fortified cliff dwellings. Rocky Mountain survivors became Utes, Shoshones, and Comanche.

Another ice age followed, lasting hundreds of years. The humans, plants, and animals that survived the cold are the same as we see today.

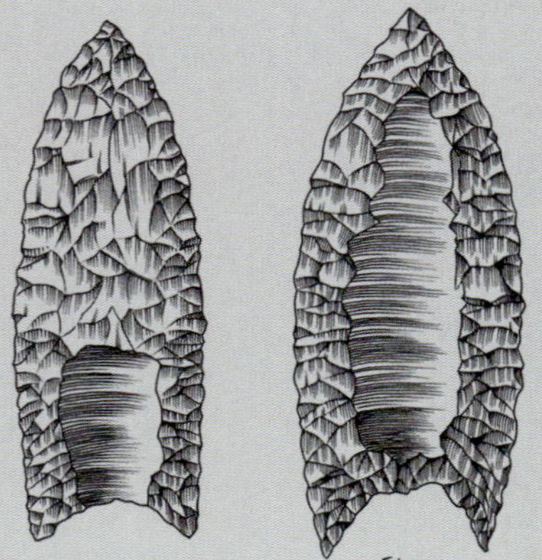

Thrusting Spear

The thrusting spear is the earliest known weapon used by humans.

Early humans used spears to hunt woolly mammoths, giant bison and other animals.

Animal sinew was used to tie a stone point to a long wooden shaft. This spear was capable of penetrating tough hides, but had to be thrust from close range.

Such close encounters were quite dangerous. Archeologists have likened the skeletal injuries of prehistoric Indians to those of modern rodeo cowboys suffering major trauma from large animals.

FROM TOP: *Clovis Spearhead, Folsom Spearhead, Flint Dagger*

MURAL NOTES

Where No Man Had Gone Before

Original Artwork by H. C. Zachry

"I wanted the mural to show how meager the resources for survival were for the Clovis culture some 15,000 years ago—and what they faced in order to live through each day. The wooly mammoths were often 10 feet high at the shoulder—double the height of the hunter. For this group (the first documented Americans), armed only with spears, an encounter with a mammoth, giant bison or saber-toothed cat put them nose to nose with eternity. I painted to convey the feeling of those disheartening confrontations. Other than some possible genetics, the only surviving remainders of these hardy people are their unique stone spear points. Clovis Man was the first mural I painted, and in it I developed the color palette that would be used in all the murals."

—H. C. Zachry

Paint Rock

For hundreds of years nomadic Indians carved or painted messages on rocks above the Concho River, about 70 miles south of Abilene.

More than 1500 petroglyphs and pictographs cover about a half-mile of a limestone cliff, now called Paint Rock.

Some of the artwork was created as early as 1300 A.D., but other drawings were done as recently as the 1700s and 1800s.

The drawings depict star arrangements that adorned the heavens centuries ago, as well as battles and historic events.

These cultural and creative expressions help us better understand how these various tribes—some of whom disappeared long ago—saw themselves and their world.

Ancient Bone Punches and Awls

MURAL NOTES

Signs of the Times

Original Art by H. C. Zachry

"Nomadic cultures crossed West Texas through the centuries, seeking wood, water and animals. A favorite camp was Paint Rock, an escarpment near a river about 70 miles from Abilene. These groups made hundreds of rock paintings to illustrate actual events as well as various beliefs or observations important to their group. Amazingly, you can see paintings of events by these "uncivilized" peoples that match what can be found in our classroom history books. The earliest drawings were made around 700 years ago. As I sketched on a theme for this mural, a concept emerged to remind us that communication between West Texans —now centered on Twitter, Google and other electronic marvels, started with a simple berry-stained handprint on a flat rock. The symbols I painted are copied directly from Paint Rock, though the characters are generic."

—H. C. Zachry

"But there is beauty here, the beauty of space and of freedom, and the beauty of the wind feeling its way along the brown, grassy swells and ruffling the yellow ridges."

—A. C. Greene, Abilene native and Texas writer

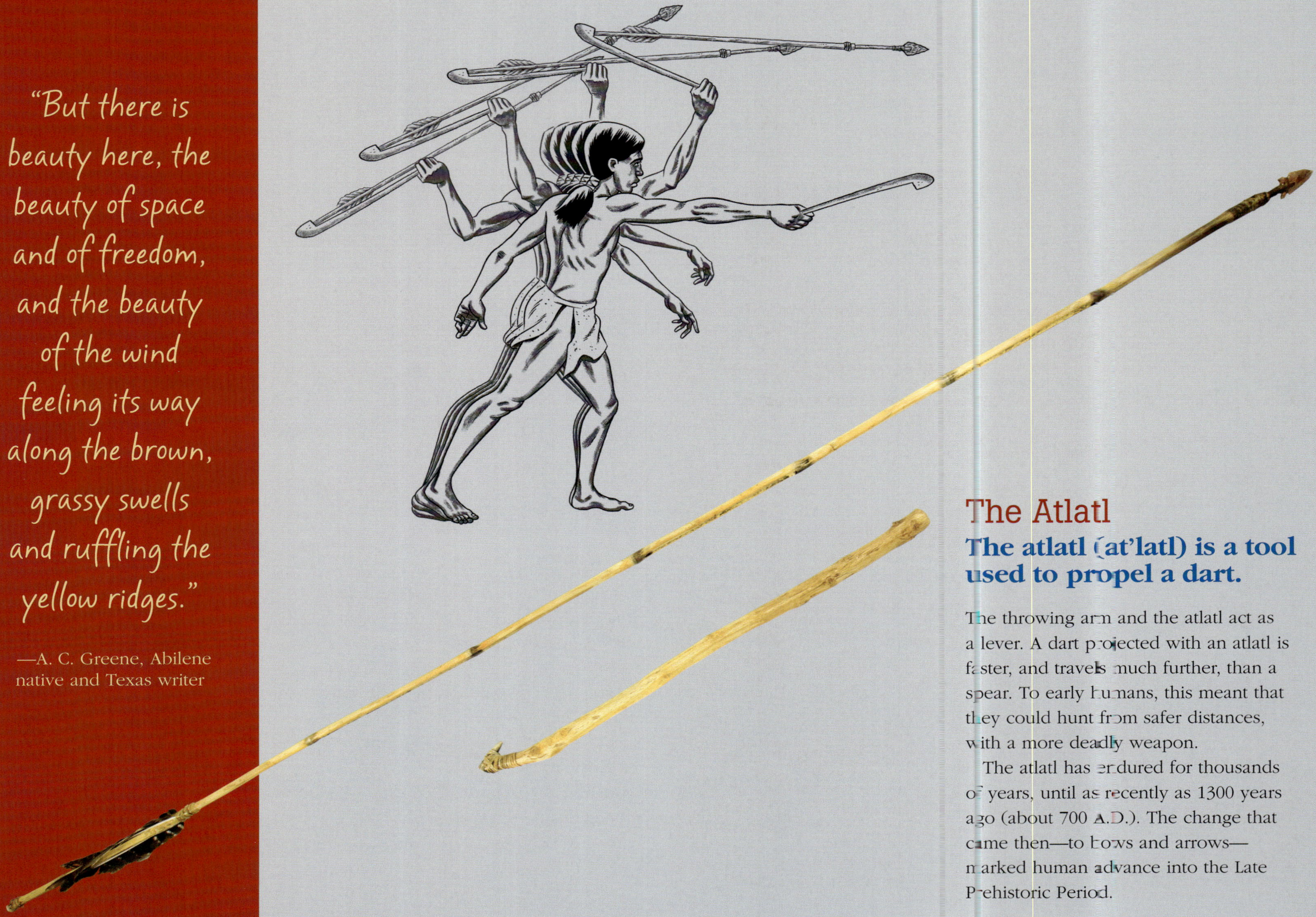

The Atlatl

The atlatl (at'latl) is a tool used to propel a dart.

The throwing arm and the atlatl act as a lever. A dart projected with an atlatl is faster, and travels much further, than a spear. To early humans, this meant that they could hunt from safer distances, with a more deadly weapon.

The atlatl has endured for thousands of years, until as recently as 1300 years ago (about 700 A.D.). The change that came then—to bows and arrows—marked human advance into the Late Prehistoric Period.

The Jumano and Apache

Over the centuries, transient cultures sometimes survived climate changes only to be displaced by stronger or more warlike tribes.

Two of the more recent cultures in this human revolving door were the Jumano and the Apache. The Jumano were here until about 400 years ago. They were skilled traders in buffalo meat and hides, and had established a trade network that reached from East Texas to the Pueblos of New Mexico.

Around 1600 A.D. the more hostile Apache Indians displaced the Jumano. The Apache were also nomadic, carrying their tipis and belongings on travois pulled by dogs.

In 1724 Comanches attacked Apache villages on the Big Wichita River, thereby completing their expulsion of the Apache from West Texas.

Stone arrow tips

TOP: *Metal-tipped arrow*

BOTTOM: *Leather-handled battle axe*

MURAL NOTES

When Discovery Means Death

Original Art by H. C. Zachry

"The violence of the displacement of various cultures is the early story of this land. One tribe or group killed or chased another tribe or group out of the area, time and time again. In this mural, I wanted to show the feeling of doom that members of a weaker culture would feel upon seeing an endless new procession of stronger people, coming to conquer. The tribes are generic, but representative. For example, around 1600, the Apaches destroyed the resident Jumano Indian culture, only to be themselves driven out a century later."

—H. C. Zachry

Bows and Arrows

The bow and arrow extended the distance between the hunter and his prey even more than the atlatl.

Hunting or fighting was less likely to result in injury, and more likely to result in a kill. Indians began to use the bow and arrow about 1300 years ago. Initially, the weapons were rather crude, but within a few hundred years they had become quite advanced.

On the Texas frontier, the bow and arrow prevailed as the leading firepower until the revolving pistol was developed in the mid-1800s.

MURAL NOTES

Home Sweet Home

Original Art by H. C. Zachry

"My assignment was to illustrate the permanence of the Comanche settling here, after destroying the last Apache stronghold in Texas. The Comanche had gained horses, which allowed them to raid and hunt at will—and to live permanently in this area. All preceding groups had been largely nomadic. Comanche moved their villages around, but it was all their land. I wanted to show the existence of horses, as well as the relaxed mood of the tribe in their permanent homes. It was an attractive country to those who could survive here, so I wanted the mural to also convey the beauty of the region."

—H. C. Zachry

The First Permanent Occupants

The Comanche Indians, mounted on horses, were the first group to claim this region as home.

Around 1700 A.D. the acquisition of horses catapulted the Comanche from a small tribe to a feared race of skilled hunters, savvy traders and merciless enemies.

On horseback, the Comanche could hunt, raid, and trade over hundreds of miles.

They soon dominated the territory that extended from western Oklahoma, across the Texas Panhandle, and into New Mexico.

After 15,000 years the Texas frontier was finally permanent home to a culture.

The Plains Buffalo

In 1800, more than 40 million bison roamed the plains of the American West.

For thousands and thousands of years, Indian survival depended on the plentiful buffalo. It provided them with food, shelter, and clothing.

For some tribes, the buffalo was the spiritual center of their life, believed to be a gift from the Great Spirit.

Comanche legend tells us that each spring the buffalo emerged from great caves in the earth.

Buffalo were well-equipped to protect themselves from natural predators, including wolves, but not from man.

"Soon we saw a cloud of dust rising. We judged the herd to be five or six miles wide. As far as we could see was a seemingly solid mass of buffaloes."

—Nathaniel Langford, circa 1870

Buffalo Bulls Fighting in Rutting Season *by George Catlin, 1836*
National Museum of American Art, Smithsonian Institute

Horses Change Everything

Spanish explorers, priests and settlers introduced horses to the New World.

Spanish explorers first crossed this region in 1528–1545. Later, Spanish priests and settlers established communities in New Mexico. For 100 years, the Spanish dominated the Pueblo Indians there.

But in 1680 the Indians revolted, killing hundreds of settlers. About 3000 Spaniards fled, abandoning most of their horses and livestock. The Pueblo Indians traded the captured horses to the Utes and Comanche living to the north in the Rocky Mountains.

The Comanche saw the horse as a way to hunt, trade and make war at will. They began increasing their herds by breeding and raiding from other tribes.

In 1706 only Comanche men were seen on horseback. Within a decade every Comanche man, woman and child was riding a horse.

Coronado Sets Out to the North *by Frederick Remington*

Spanish Exploration

Spanish explorers were the first Europeans to set foot in Texas.

Around 1530 Cabeza de Vaca and four survivors, shipwrecked at Galveston Bay, marched through Texas in search of gold. De Vaca later bragged about legends of seven cities of gold, Cíbola.

In 1540 Spain sent Francisco Vásquez de Coronado, with 1500 men and 1500 horses, to search for the golden cities. He would find no gold, but the Spanish presence in Texas was now established.

Two hundred years later, the Spanish sent a Frenchman, Pierre (Pedro) Vial, to repair relationships with the Indians. Vial documented a route between San Antonio and Santa Fe, New Mexico, making him the first European to map the Texas Panhandle region.

RIGHT: *Pedro Vial maps route between San Antonio and Santa Fe, 1787*

Spanish Colonization

The Spanish established missions, presidios, and towns, to secure their holdings in the Southwest.

Santa Cruz de San Saba

In 1757 Spaniards built the Mission Santa Cruz de San Saba to convert Apache Indians to Catholicism. Comanche warriors, fearing such alliances, destroyed the mission.

In the late 1600s and early 1700s, the Spanish built missions north of the Rio Grande. To protect these religious settlements, they constructed presidios (forts). Later, Spanish settlers created the first towns, called pueblos.

Through the missions, Spanish priests hoped to convert Native Americans to Catholicism.

Presidios, manned by a small number of soldiers, protected the settlements. Like the missions, the presidios helped the Spanish control its lands north of the Rio Grande.

The Spanish government offered free land to settle in San Antonio de Béxar, one of the best-known early settlements. Indian attacks, droughts, floods and disease killed many settlers.

The First Anglos

In the early 1800s, the Spanish government encouraged non-Spanish settlers to come to this region to create a buffer against the constant Comanche raids.

Early Texas organizers, like Stephen F. Austin, were given the title of Empressario and the rights to huge land grants from the Spanish government, which allowed them to entice Anglo settlers with offers of free land.

With the offer of free land, organizers recruited Americans from the east, as well as European groups, to settle these land grants.

Because of the vastness of the area, and the lack of organized government, there was often conflict between new settlers and people loyal to the Spanish government—in addition to the constant Indian conflicts.

To help protect the settlers, Stephen F. Austin formed the Texas Rangers. But, these conflicts eventually led to Texas' war for independence from Mexico, culminating in Texian victory at San Jacinto in 1836.

TEXAS

FOREVER!!

The usurper of the South has failed in his efforts to enslave the freemen of Texas.

The wives and daughters of Texas will be saved from the brutality of Mexican soldiers.

Now is the time to emigrate to the Garden of America.

A free passage, and all found, is offered at New Orleans to all applicants. Every settler receives a location of

EIGHT HUNDRED ACRES OF LAND.

LEFT: *1836 advertisement for purchasing land in Texas.*

BELOW: *Illustration of Early Anglo Settlers by Andy Simmons.*

There's More to the Story

Touch-Screen Interactive Content

Historical content available on interactive touch-screens covers six cultures, with four layers of detailed information and visuals available about each.

WHO
LIVED
HERE?
THE JUMANO
circa 1500
WHEN EUROPEANS ARRIVED in the Americas, they discovered an amazing array of cultures. The Jumano lived as semi-nomadic traders, carrying goods between the Pueblo in present-day New Mexico, the Patarabueye in the Big Bend Region, the Wichita up north, and the Caddo in present-day East Texas — crisscrossing Frontier Texas.
WHERE DID THEY GO?
WHERE DID THEY LIVE?
ELSEWHERE IN THE WORLD
Before People
First People
The Ancestors
Jumano
Apache
Comanche

WHO
LIVED
HERE?
THE APACHE
1528-1700
AMONG GROUPS THAT immigrated to the Americas from Asia were Athapaskan-speaking peoples who spread out over the interior of Alaska and Northwest Canada. Centuries later, some immigrated further south driving away populations in their path. By 1600 the Spanish referred to these newcomers as *apaches*, a Pueblo word for *enemy*.
WHERE DID THEY GO?
WHERE DID THEY LIVE?
ELSEWHERE IN THE WORLD
Before People
The Ancestors
Apache
Comanche

WHO
LIVED
HERE?
THE COMANCHE
1720-1878
THE COMANCHES EMERGED from west of the southern Rocky Mountains in the early 1700s and, recognizing the value of horses and their usefulness for extensive raiding and trading networks, dominated Frontier Texas for the next 150 years. They prospered as they became peerless horse, hide, and captive traders.
WHERE DID THEY GO?
WHERE DID THEY LIVE?
ELSEWHERE IN THE WORLD
Before People
First People
The Ancestors
Jumano
Apache

CHAPTER 2

Comanche Empire

How the small Comanche tribe rose from obscurity to dominate a huge part of the Southwest for almost 200 years.

From the early 1700s to the late 1800s, the Comanche Indians dominated the Southern Plains.

Riding on recently acquired horses, the Comanche hunted, traded, and made war across a huge expanse of the Southwest.

Mobility, as well as economic and militaristic supremacy, made them the first culture to sustain dominance of the frontier Texas region.

The Comanche were formidable enough to block European expansion into their homeland for over 150 years, a feat no other Native American tribe achieved.

The tribe called themselves *Numunah*, simply "Our People." The Spanish, however, called this region *Comancheria*—the Comanche Empire.

Satanta
Kiowa Chief

Nakoney
Comanche—
Son of Horse-Back

Horse-Back
Comanche Chief—
Nakoney Band

Ho-we-ah
Comanche Chief

Esihabitu (Asa-Harvey)
Comanche Chief

"A stake of about four feet was driven into the ground. Upon the top of this was placed the bloody scalp of my sister, Emma. The brown locks that once lay so loose and wavy are now matted together with crimson clots and presented a most horrible appearance. Around these warriors danced, shrieked, and yelled most hideously, waving the gory garments my sister wore at the time of her death."

—Anna Metzger, captive of the Kiowa Indians

The Comanche were exceptional horsemen.

They were able to hunt buffalo astride their horse at high speeds, using long spears or bows and arrows.

The Comanche depended upon specially trained horses to navigate the dangers of the hunt, which could easily bring death or serious injury.

MURAL NOTES

High-Risk Groceries

Original Artwork by H. C. Zachry

"To introduce the Comanche Section, we wanted to show the tight link between the Comanche and their horses as well as their interplay with the buffalo, the major source of food. The layout of the exhibit required the mural to be in a vertical format, which was a bit challenging at first. After some sketching, the rearing horse concept emerged and then it was pretty easy to fill the picture with action and to reflect the dangers involved in going after the buffalo with a spear. This was not an activity for timid men."

—H. C. Zachry

Authentic buffalo headdress made of hide, horn and hoof chips.

"We all opened fire on them. Three of the bucks went down, when the squaw . . . emptied two six-shooters at us, but none of the shots took effect. Then, jumping from her horse, she clasped her hands on her breasts shouting 'me squaw, me squaw' thinking she could get off because she was a woman. Someone shot her in the stomach, as a squaw horse thief wasn't considered any better than a buck horse thief. Another well-aimed shot put an end to her. I skinned the squaw. We tanned these Indian hides afterwards and I made a purse out of the squaw's belly."

—Jim McIntire, Texas cowboy, buffalo hunter, lawman and ranger

Comanche Economic Empire

The Comanche built an economic empire by controlling trade with the Spanish, other tribes, and eventually with American traders.

The Comanche traded with New Mexican traders, called *Comancheros*, at trade fairs such as the one at Taos. After a 1780 treaty with New Mexico, they began to trade along the Caprock escarpment in the Texas Panhandle.

By using diplomacy, trade and violence, the *Numunah* elbowed all other Indians out of the South Plains and even blocked the Europeans, except when it suited them to do otherwise.

Comanches soon reduced Santa Fe and San Antonio to near dependency on their commerce and personal whims.

The Comanche controlled trade for over 100 years, but as more and more settlers moved onto the frontier, and Indian attacks increased, settlers called on the government to end the trade.

Comancheria Map, 1780–1820

MURAL NOTES

I Came, Saw, Conquered

Original Art by H. C. Zachry

"Empire! I was told to convey a feeling of grandeur, of supremacy for the Comanche. They deserved it, because they ruled a huge region of the Southwest for 200 years with an iron fist. So, I was looking for a pose that reflected dominance, of supreme confidence. I did the single Indian because the Comanche outlook was so singular. Every warrior had to earn his own stripes. He was free to change from one band to another, anytime. Each was thoroughly independent, honoring leaders, agreements and customs as it suited him. I tried to convey that solitary, authoritarian attitude." —*H. C. Zachry*

"A Comanche on horseback, with his lance and shield by his side, is beautifully classic."

—First Lieutenant T. B. Wheelock, 1st U. S. Dragoons.

The initial success of the *Comanchero* trade came because of merchandise the Comanche could use in their everyday pursuits.

ABOVE: *22" metal hand axe*
15" metal hand axe
Hand axes were useful in everything from cutting firewood to skinning buffalo.

RIGHT: *Trade beads*
The Comanche Indians considered ornamentation a mark of prestige and experience. *Comancheros* traded jewelry and clothing such as these throughout their century of commerce with the Comanche.

LEFT: *Trade whiskey jug*
Cooking pot
Comancheros began using oxcarts (carretas) to trade a wider variety of items. The addition of whiskey, guns, and especially human captives, contributed to their increasingly negative reputation.

"These parties of Comancheros... launch upon the plains with a few trinkets... which they barter away to the savages for horses and mules."
--Josiah Gregg, frontiersman, 1844

Comanche Currency: Captives, Hides and Horses

Comanches traded captives, hides and horses in exchange for manufactured goods, arms and ammunition.

Having first obtained captured Spanish horses from the Pueblo Indians, Comanches soon developed a vigorous horse trade business with other Plains tribes. To meet demands, they raided horses from New Mexico, northern Mexico and Texas.

Raiding warriors often killed the elderly and very young, taking the able-bodied as captives to be sold to *Comanchero* traders, whom they met along the Caprock in West Texas. The *Comancheros* then sold or ransomed the captives in the Santa Fe slave market.

In the quest for horses and captives, thousands of people were killed and hundreds more disappeared into the great abyss of *Comancheria*.

MURAL NOTES

Making the Cash Register Ring

Original Art by H. C. Zachry

"The Comanche were all about business—hunting, raiding and trading. Few other Indians equaled them in their trading endeavors. Their first big business was selling horses to other Plains tribes—Sioux, Cheyenne, Kiowa and others. The Comanche had gained horses from the Navaho, who had kept them as booty after they killed all the Spanish in New Mexico or chased them back to El Paso in 1680. The second big phase of commerce was the buffalo hide trade—a modest activity that helped meet the Spanish/Anglo need for heavy clothing and blankets. The biggest Comanche venture and the one that ultimately led to their destruction (after almost 100 years) was the trade in human captives. They grabbed women and children in Texas, Mexico and New Mexico and sold or traded them to other Indians, Comancheros *and the Spanish. In these small paintings, I tried to show the anticipation of the sellers and buyers doing 'the deal'—as well as the less joyous plight of the products being sold."*

—H. C. Zachry

"They seemed to like Mexican captives, because when they brought them in they could raise them up and no one could tell them from full blood Indians."

—Jeff Smith, Comanche captive

Making the Cash Register Ring

1. Tanned buffalo hides were initially traded at the Taos Trade Fair to use as rugs and lap robes.

2. The Comanche were the primary suppliers of an ever-growing demand for horses among other Indian tribes.

3. Captives were sold to the Comancheros in the Valley of Tears near the present-day town of Quitaque.

1

2

3

Esihabitu is portrayed by Richard Ray Whitman, who has appeared in movies such as Indian Graffiti, Lakota Woman, My Heroes Have Always Been Cowboys *and* Oklahoma Passage.

Spirit Guide

Esihabitu

Esihabitu was a visionary Comanche leader whose life spanned early days on the warpath to meeting the President in Washington, D. C. That meeting convinced him that the war with the Whites couldn't be won and he worked for a peaceful resolution. He was known from the Red River to the Hill Country, first as a raider and later as one who would negotiate the return of captives from various Indian bands. He inscribed his signature as a pictograph at Paint Rock, where it can be seen today.

My People

"Haa haits"! Hello, friend.

Since long. long ago, Indians have come to the banks of the Concho River—which we call "ebi hunubi" or Blue River—to camp, because it gives us water, wood, and a long rock cliff to protect us from the wind. While they were camped here, the Indians used paints to tell their stories on the cliffs of Paint Rock. In this place are stories, some from tribes and languages long forgotten, pictures of the old ways, hunting the buffalo in the time before the horse, stalking him on foot with bow and arrow . . . talking to the sun, Our Father, and asking for puha, the medicine power that makes us strong.

The paintings here and at other places on the Plains were drawn to remind us of our stories. We made no written words. OUR stories are passed from generation to generation by word of mouth. From old to young we tell these stories in the long nights of winter at places like this one, places that breathe with the history of our people.

White Conflict

Haa, tell me some good news, brother!

The Taibos, or Whites, know my tribe as the Comanches, but since the beginning of time, we called ourselves the Numunah, which means "all of us," or Our People. We were always hunters and warriors, and once we became the masters of horses we grew in numbers and strength, and we took the Plains of Texas as our own.

Our People fought bravely to keep the Spanish soldiers and priests from marking the Plains with their footprints. The Numunah also blocked the Mexicans and the French. The Texans too—for almost 100 winters we kept them from claiming our lands. Nobody crossed West Texas unless we willed it.

I do not yet know the end of this story between the Numunah and the Whites, but even if the day comes when we no longer live free, we should be remembered with respect for our way of living.

Facing Tomorrow

In my time, even as Our People are put on reservations or retreat into the canyons of the High Plains, the paintings on the rocks—and the stories they tell—are still being made.

We paint newer pictures among the ancient ones, showing how our paths cross with the paths of the Whites.

Back in my grandfather's time, the Comanches rode with the Wichitas to burn the spirit house of the taibos at San Saba River, what we call tsuku kahni hunubi (pron. tsookoo connee hoonoov), "old house river," because the ruins are still there. But the taibos have another big spirit house south of here at the place they call San Antonio.

Those taibos believe in a bad spirit who looks like a white man with horns and a tail, who tells them to do bad things. Sometimes I think maybe all taibos listen too much to their bad spirit.

Yes, we have fought to keep our land and way of life. But I see that our old ways of raiding and taking captives must change. Now I try to stop these things among Our People, and I tell them to give the captives back. I cannot decide this by myself. We must have a council with a great many speeches and we must all agree. Everyone. Now I argue for peace with the Whites, but I do not want us to become like the Whites ourselves. . . .

Comanche at War

Comanche warriors were fearless, had great endurance, and neither gave nor expected mercy.

The Comanche had learned to fight from horseback, making them superior warriors. They were greatly respected as fighters and dreaded as captors.

Before 1700, Indian arrowheads and spear points were made of stone. Later, raiding and trade networks supplied metal, which could be cut into iron points—creating a more enduring lethal weapon.

The Comanche eagerly consumed guns, either by trade or stolen on raids. But they often were useless in battle as a result of mismatched ammunition or lack of maintenance.

The Comanche population increased from about 1500 in 1720 to over 40,000 in 1780, more than the combined Anglo and Spanish populations in the Southwest.

Comanche Mounted War Party *by George Catlin, 183[illegible]*
National Museum of American Art, Smithsonian Institute

"Suddenly, the war whoop of the Comanche burst upon our ears sending terror to all hearts. My father, in trying to reach the house for weapons, was shot down, and near him my mother, clinging to her children and praying God to spare them, was also murdered, and as she pressed us to her heart we were baptized in her precious blood."

—Rebecca J. Gilleland Fisher, pioneer

The piece above is a replica of ledger art created by the Kiowa artist, Silverhorns, in the 1880s. It depicts "The Exploits of Sun Boy."

The Exploits of Sun Boy

Plains Indians adopted cloth, paper, pencils and commercial paint as they became available from traders, and used them to create pictographs. Each picture was a reminder of a story to be told orally. The style is called "ledger art" after bank ledger books, a common source of paper.

1. Sun Boy Killing an Osage Warrior

The Osage warrior is wearing a roach headdress and black moccasins. Most likely, Sun Boy killed the warrior to revenge the 1833 Cutthroat massacre. Osages had killed and decapitated Kiowas camped north of the Red River, leaving their heads in camp buckets.

2. Sun Boy Fighting Mexican Soldiers

Sun Boy braves a hail of bullets fired by a line of Mexican soldiers, recognizable by their blue coats and brimmed hats. Such a skirmish may have occurred during Kiowa raids into Mexico.

3. Sun Boy Fighting the Pawnees

The Pawnee of Nebraska, in brightly colored shirts, were traditional enemies of the Kiowa. This scene likely refers to a fight in 1851 when the Kiowa defeated some Pawnees who had stolen a flag from the Kiowa's sun dance lodge.

4. Sun Boy Fights the U. S. Army

This scene may illustrate a skirmish in 1869 with troops under Captain Curwen B. McClelland out of Fort Richardson (near Jacksboro), following the robbery of a mail coach at Rock Station, Texas, by chief Kicking Bird.

5. Sun Boy Encounters General William T. Sherman

In 1871 Kiowa warriors, laying in ambush above a wagon train in Young County, allowed General Sherman's inspection party to pass unharmed. Hours later they attacked the wagon train, killing seven drivers. Sun Boy is shown here counting coup (touching, not killing) with an army officer.

6. A Texan is Killed

In 1878 Texas Rangers killed Sun Boy's brother while the Kiowa band was hunting buffalo near Quanah, Texas. The next year another brother claimed revenge, ambushing a Texan named Joe Earle. This was the last Kiowa raid into Texas.

Comanche Life

The Comanche tribe was a collection of small bands.

Comanche bands were groups of extended family lines that supported each other in hunting, trading and fighting.

Affiliation was voluntary, and individuals and families often drifted between bands. Leaders were those who could command respect and bring prosperity. Some bands numbered in the dozens, others in the thousands.

Men were hunters, traders and fighters. Women did the daily chores, including transporting and erecting the heavy buffalo hide tipis.

Women had little status. Men usually considered horses as their most valuable property, then their dogs, then their wives and children.

Indian Village on the Move
Charles M. Russell, 1905
National Archives

MURAL NOTES

Moonrise

Original Art by H. C. Zachry

"This was the last mural painted. We felt that something was needed that showed the quiet side of Indian life—their daily existence. I painted a scene set at night in order to concentrate on just the camp and tipis. At first, I put the inhabitants outside. But the idea emerged to place people inside the tents and let the viewer see them in an unusual way, as only silhouettes and shadows. I thought this made the static scene more exciting and dramatic. The process also reflects the nature of exhibit work—after all my planning for the impact of a giant picture showing this speck of life within the vast Texas wilderness—most of the mural was ultimately hidden by an adjacent exhibit installation. Such is life."

—H. C. Zachry

Decline of an Empire

By the late 19th century the Comanche Empire had been reduced from a powerful force to a small group of starving Indians.

Several factors contributed to the decline of the Comanche Empire. A nomadic lifestyle and heavy protein diet had reduced fertility. Child mortality was high.

Smallpox, introduced by Spanish explorers, killed off 80% of some Indian populations. Later epidemics of smallpox and cholera would continue to ravage the Comanche in 1781, 1816, 1848, 1849 and 1851.

Relentless waves of settlers in the 19th century destroyed Comanche hunting grounds and the buffalo.

In 1836 there were 40,000 Texans and non-Indians, and 30,000 Comanche. By 1880 no Comanche were left in Texas. Instead, 1,600,000 Texans occupied the state.

Quah-ah-da Comanche camp, photographed by W. S. Soule Center for American History, The University of Texas Austin

"My band is not going to live on the reservation. Tell the white chiefs that the Quahadi are warriors."

—Quanah Parker, 1867

Cynthia Ann and Quanah Parker

In 1836 Comanches attacked Parker's Fort in central Texas and captured ten-year-old Cynthia Ann. For 25 years Cynthia lived as Comanche. She married Chief Peta Nocona and had three children. In 1860 the Texas Rangers recaptured her in north Texas and returned her to the Parker family. But these people were no longer her family—she was Comanche. Within a few years she died of grief.

Her oldest son, Quanah, was born about 1845. He later became chief of the most warlike band of Comanches, the Quahadi. Long after other tribes were on the reservation, the Quahadi continued to live on the Plains—hunting, raiding and fighting.

But by 1876 relentless pressure from the Army forced the starving Quahadi to an Oklahoma reservation, where Quanah became the most influential Comanche of the reservation era.

Cynthia Ann Parker, and baby "Prairie Flower," the mother and sister of Chief Quanah Parker, in 1860,--soon after her re-capture by the rangers.

FAR LEFT: *Chief Quanah Parker, the most famous Indian on the Texas frontier, was the son of a white captive, Cynthia Ann Parker* (NEAR LEFT).

"If the Texans had kept out of my country, there might have been peace. The Texans have taken away the places where the grass grew the thickest and the timber was the best. I was born upon the prairie where the wind blew free; we only wish to wander on the plains until we die."

—Ten Bears, Yamparika Comanche

Satanta is portrayed by Azgad Crisostomo, a character actor in several movies.

Spirit Guide

Satanta

One of the most aggressive warriors on the Texas Frontier, Satanta, also known as Settainte, or White Bear, was a Kiowa Chief. Satanta abhorred the tragedies being inflicted upon his people and saw no honor in trying to negotiate peace with whites. In 1867 the *New York Times* wrote "in cunning or native diplomacy Satanta has no equal in boldness, daring and merciless cruelty." Larry McMurtrey's character Blue Duck in *Lonesome Dove* was loosely modeled after this fierce Indian leader.

My People

We are warriors—from the beginning and to the end. If white people do not know this, they do not know the Kiowa, or our brothers, the Comanche.

How else can a boy become a man, unless he fights, unless he is willing to give up his life for our people? If he shows that he will die before giving up, he is "kluk tsingta", a true horse, one who never gives up.

Our great chiefs have all been warriors. They have proven themselves in battle and brought honor to our people. I am a chief because I fight.

They say I have killed more white people than any other Indian on the plains.

I hope it's true.

White Conflict

Every treaty with the white man is a mistake. They will not live by their treaties, and we cannot live by them.

If they tell me where I can live, where I can hunt, that is not our way. If I am a man, I must be free.

If I cannot hunt buffalo... How will we eat? They bring cattle to the reservation, but the cattle are poor. They are hardly worth butchering.

Sometimes they bring meat. But it is rotten. It is crawling with maggots. We cannot live like this.

And they say, "you must only live on this land," but "this land" gets smaller and smaller because the white pests keep coming. This is not as they said it would be. Many Indian and white chiefs met at Medicine Lodge. I signed a treaty there. I know now this is also a bad treaty.

Now there is no doubt. To make a treaty with a white man is weakness. They only take away. They do not give. If we want to live, there is only one path. The warpath.

Facing Tomorrow

I will never make peace with the whites. Living as they wish us to live is to die slowly.

I have spent many days in the white man's prisons. But I will tell you, a reservation is also a prison. So I make war on the whites.

Some of my brothers say, "Do not do this. And if you must make war, do it in secret, and keep your victories secret." But there is no honor in such secrets.

I speak proudly of my fights. I am a warrior. A warrior's victories are a warrior's honor. My people will make new songs about how we slaughtered the white invaders.

Now, I hear the army is coming for me. Once again, they will arrest me. They will take my body just as they take everything. But they can never take my heart.

Buffalo Hide Tipi and Furnishings

The Comanche and other Plains Indians lived in tipis that could be quickly assembled and disassembled. About 20 buffalo hides, weighing 200 pounds, were sewn together and attached to poles. Many of the items they needed for their day-to-day life were also made from hide, as well as other parts of the buffalo.

1. *Buffalo Hide Berry Pounding Bowl and Stone Pounder*
2. *Buffalo shoulder Blade Plates*
3. *Painted Par Fleche Storage Bags*
4. *Dried Buffalo Stomach Cooker*
5. *Beaded Bags for Clothing*
6. *Wooden Bowls and Buffalo Horn Spoons*
7. *Back Rest Chairs*
8. *Painted Rawhide Utility Bags*
9. *Buffalo Bladder Water Bag*
10. *War Shield*
11. *Metal-tipped Lance*
12. *Pad Saddle*
13. *Quirt with Beaded Strap*
14. *Carved Tipi Pegs and Lacing Pins*
15. *Horse Hair Rope*
16. *Fire for Cooking and Heat*
17. *Buffalo Leather Robe*
18. *Painted Tipi Liner*

LEFT: *War Shield*

9
10
5
5
11
8
8
8
4
18
7
7
3
3
17
13
12
6
14
2
15
6
16
1

"One of the boys was shot in the forehead with an arrow tipped with a steel spike, which drove through his skull and deep into his head. In trying to pull the arrow out, he broke it off. They found in trying to extract the spike that to pull on it would tear open the head bone and result in instant death, so with Divine faith they left nature to take its course. After carrying the arrow spike in this way for eight weeks, by the help of nature, the bone slackened its grip on the spike until it was slipped out. He lived many years afterwards to be a prosperous citizen."

—G. A. Holland, county historian and mayor of Weatherford, Texas

There's More to the Story

See pages 140–145 for information on these topics:

Buffalo and Early Indians

- Ancient Origins
- Bountiful Buffalo
- Cultural Remnants
- Early Indian Images

Tribes of the Region

- The Comanches
- The Kiowas
- Delawares, Kickapoos, and Tonkawas
- Warfare and Ceremony

Indians and Horses

- Mounting Up
- Extraordinary Equestrians
- Riding Equipment
- Wealth and Status

The information available in There's More to the Story *following most chapters in this book is from the Rotators, which are wall-mounted rotating information-centers throughout Frontier Texas! The Rotators contain a great deal more information about each subject.*

Buffalo Trade

The frontier's first economic boom involved both winners and losers.

CHAPTER 3

The discovery that buffalo hides were suitable for industrial leather created an industry that transformed frontier Texas.

Soon after the Civil War, eastern capitalists ordered as many buffalo hides as could be supplied. Hunters responded, first decimating the herds on the Northern Plains, and then coming after the millions of Texas buffalo.

A government treaty protected the Texas buffalo for Indians, but hunters ignored it. The military "looked the other way" as the loss of buffalo would force the Indians onto reservations.

Texas buffalo were killed out in less than a decade.

The Man Who Started it All

J. Wright Mooar saw an economic opportunity—and launched an industry.

Around 1870 J. Wright Mooar was hunting buffalo to feed railroad crews in Kansas when he sent about 30 hides to his brother in New York to see if they would make good leather.

A tannery conducted some experiments, concluding that the hides would indeed be ideal for industrial use. An order was placed for 4000 hides. It was like winning the lottery!

Wright, now joined by his brother, began killing buffalo in earnest. The plains were soon dotted with other hunting crews.

Wright had the Sharps Arms Company make a rifle especially for buffalo hunting. Called the "Big 50," it became the gun of choice.

More than anyone else, J. Wright Mooar created and led what is now referred to as *The Great Buffalo Slaughter*. After the buffalo were gone, he ranched near Snyder, Texas.

Joseph Wright Mooar, circa 1890. Photo courtesy of Judy Hays.

> "I was making a mattress of buffalo mops. My husband would take the skin off of the front of the head that contained the long heavy mop of wool. It took two or three hundred mops, I think, but I surely had a fine mattress when it was finished."
>
> —Ella Bird Dumont, pioneer

The tools of the trade were simple, but effective.

The Sharps "Big 50" Rifle

With direction from J. Wright Mooar, the Sharps Rifle Company developed a .50-caliber rifle named the "Big 50" specifically for buffalo hunters. The hunters favored this gun because of its large caliber, accuracy and its long range. The heavy barrel helped prevent overheating from repeated firing. Indians said the 16-pound gun could "shoot today and kill tomorrow," as it could kill buffalo more than 1000 yards away.

The Most Famous Buffalo Gun in the World

This rare "Big 50" buffalo gun was owned by J. Wright Mooar. He was known to have killed more than 20,000 buffalo. This gun is perhaps the most important artifact of *The Great American Buffalo Slaughter*, an event that changed the history of western America.

This rare artifact shown through the courtesy of the Randy Hays family, descendants of J. Wright Mooar.

"The man I sold my old .44 to killed 119 buffalo in one day with it. That beats me with my Big .50—as 93 is the most that I ever killed in one day."

—R. W. Snyder, buffalo hunter, for whom Snyder, Texas is named

Mooar is portrayed by Stephen Bruton, who has had film roles in The Alamo, A Star Is Born, Heaven's Gate, Michael, Miss Congeniality, *and other movies, as well as television roles in* Matlock, Amerika, Night Stalker, *and* Murder In Travis County. *Bruton passed away in May 2009.*

Spirit Guide

J. Wright Mooar

Born in Vermont in 1851, J. Wright Mooar followed the western migration. During 1870 in Kansas, he hunted buffalo as food for the railroad crews laying track. As an experiment, he shipped two dozen buffalo hides to his brother in New York City to see if any of the area tanneries would buy them. They did, ordered more, and the great American buffalo slaughter was on. By 1876, the herds in Kansas had been exterminated. Mooar moved to Texas, using The Flat at Fort Griffin as well as Rath City as bases, and then settled in a dugout on Deep Creek as he hunted buffalo for his crews to skin. He is reputed to have killed 20,000 buffalo during his life. After the buffalo were gone, he established a ranch. Mooar's partner, Pete Snyder, had created a trading post in the area that grew into the town of Snyder, Texas.

I was just a big kid off the farm when I came to Kansas in 1870 from back East. Keeping railroad crews in meat by killing a few buffalo was a way I could make a living, so that's what I did. We sold a few hides for lap robes, but there wasn't much demand. One day, I had an idea that would change everything. I sent a few hides to my brother back in New York to see if the commercial tanneries would buy them to make leather.

Well, my gosh, it was a like finding a gold mine. He got an order for 2000 hides! He quit his job, came to Kansas, and we started killing buffalo. So did everybody else, as soon as they figured out what we was doing.

Good hunting outfits could make a lot of money. Within a year, there were hundreds of those outfits all across the Plains. We killed them shaggies by the tens of thousands...even millions, I guess. Back then, we didn't think the great buffalo herds could be wiped out. Once, I saw a herd north of here that was seven or eight miles wide—maybe a hundred miles long. There were millions of them! With 3000 buffalo hunters in Kansas it didn't take long before it seemed like there were more hunters than buffalo. I wanted to head south to Texas. We'd heard that the Medicine Lodge Treaty reserved the Texas herd for the Indians, so we went to the commanding officer of Fort Dodge, and asked what would happen to a buffalo hunter who crossed the Canadian River into Texas to hunt. "Boys," the Colonel told us "If I were a buffalo hunter I'd hunt where the buffalo are."

The government didn't say it outright, but their intention was to let us kill the buffalo in order to cripple the Indians' independence. Without buffalo, the Indians would have to live on reservations and survive on government handouts to keep from starving.

Of course, it was money to us—our livings—so with Charlie Rath and some others providing supplies, and myself, Bat Masterson and Billy Dixon leading the way, we headed for Texas. Well, the bunches of shaggies have gotten smaller and smaller—and further apart. Now I can hunt for days without seeing any buffalo. I can't afford to keep paying these skinners, if there's nothing to skin. But, buffalo led me and old Pete Snyder to this fine piece of Texas. Pete's done well as a merchant, even got a town named after him. I figure building a cattle ranch would be a good life's work for me. Without the buffalo, this grass will provide for a lot of cattle, so I'm going to give that a go. I reckon it's a good thing I hung onto the money I made.

Hunting Camps and Hide Towns

Hunting crews and hide towns brought new waves of settlers to the frontier.

Hunting teams consisted of at least four men, including a shooter and skinners. A capable man could skin 50 buffalo a day and was paid about $50 a month.

Each team killed and skinned between 50 and 100 buffalo every day.

Hide towns began to pop up across the frontier. Here, dealers purchased the hides from the hunters. They were then transported by wagon to railheads and shipped to the East.

Area hide towns included Buffalo Gap, the Flat, Fort Phantom, Snyder and Rath City. These towns were filled with stacks of hides up to 20 feet high.

These photos were taken between Abilene's site and Buffalo Gap in the 1870s. Amazingly, though the slaughter of millions of buffalo by hide hunters on the Great Plains lasted for almost a 10 year period, there are only about a dozen photographs of the entire experience. More than half the surviving photos were taken within 10 miles of Abilene.

MURAL NOTES

Rough Camp for Rough Men

Original Art by H. C. Zachry

"Cold, lonely, dangerous—groups of men, often of little prior acquaintance, were thrown together in rough buffalo hunting camps on the frontier's edge, usually for three or four months at a time. Battling the weather, Indians and backbreaking work, they did their separate jobs while going about the bloody business of gathering thousands of buffalo hides to ship East. In the mural, I wanted to show the men as a collection of individuals—to let the viewer sense their individuality, their separation from each other and from the rest of the world. I put several elements of a buffalo hide camp in plain view, as much for use by schoolteachers as anything. Cooking methods, tools, buffalo tongues, non-standard clothing and other items can be seen. This is a large mural, 24' long. It had to have things to look at all along its wall, so it was something of a challenge."

—H. C. Zachry

The hide trade involved crews of shooters and skinners.

Ammo Belt

Buffalo shooters used ammo belts to carry reloaded cartridges. They often shot more than 100 cartridges a day.

Skinning Knife Kit

Skinners kept at least two knives available and sharpened them often. An experienced man could skin 50 or more buffalo a day. Top skinners were sought after and received extra pay.

These rare frontier artifacts are shown through the courtesy of Cecil W. Brown.

BELOW: *Buffalo Hunting Ammunition Belt*

FOLLOWING PAGE: *Buffalo Skinning Knives and Case*

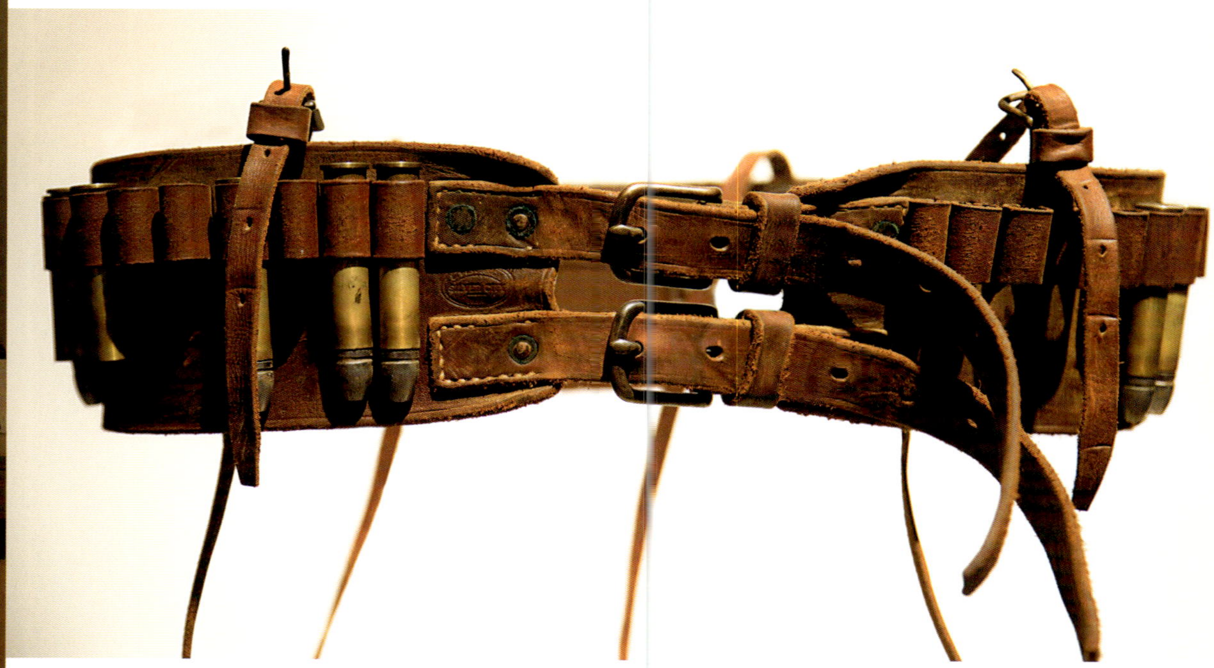

"If a herd was lying at rest,
he would pick out some buffalo
that was standing up on watch
and shoot his ball in his side
so that it would not go through.
A buffalo shot in this manner
would merely hump up his back
as if he had the colic and
commence to mill around . . .
and in this way hold the herd.
This was termed mesmerizing
the buffalo, which proved
to be the most successful way
of killing buffalo."

—W. Skelton Glenn, buffalo hunter

Buffalo Bone Trade

Buffalo bones provided a second economic boom on the frontier.

After millions of buffalo were killed, buffalo bones covered the prairie. It was said that you could walk the 15 miles from Abilene to Buffalo Gap on buffalo bones without touching the ground.

In the 1880s drought and a national recession hit settlers hard. To help save their farms and businesses, they gathered tons and tons of bones from the prairies and hauled them in wagons to railroad boneyards.

The bones were then shipped east to make buttons, corset stays, fertilizer and fuel for the furnaces used to fire bone china.

Buffalo bones were piled for rail shipment on the very spot in Abilene where you are standing—the first commercial use of this site.

AT RIGHT: *Buffalo bone pile at Frontier Texas!*

FACING PAGE: Gathering Buffalo Bones, *Dickinson Research Center, National Cowboy & Western Heritage Museum*

Buffalo math

Number of American bison in North America before the Plains Indians acquired horses—between 30 million and 60 million

Number of American bison killed in Kansas and Texas between 1868 and 1881—between 20 million and 31 million

Number of American bison in the United States in 1889—541

Number of American bison in North America today—150,000 to 200,000

596

Cynthia Parker is portrayed by Amy Jones, who has performed in commercials, movies and TV in programs such as The Practice, History's Mysteries *and* Resurrection Blvd.

Spirit Guide

Cynthia Ann Parker

Cynthia Ann Parker was only 10 or 11 years old living at Fort Parker in Limestone County when a large group of Indians raided the fort, killing several people and taking five captives, including Cynthia. She remained with the Comanches for the next 25 years and married Peta Nocona, a respected warrior. They had three children, one of whom would become the great chief Quanah Parker. In a battle on the Pease River in 1860, several members of her band were killed and she and two Comanches were captured in a raid by Texas Rangers, who believed at first that she was an Indian, but then saw her blue eyes. She was eventually returned to her family and Anglo life, which she resented and resisted. Her small daughter, Topsanna, died. Cynthia made several attempts to return to the Comanches but was made to live in a world she didn't know or like until her death, about three years after her capture.

"Haa haits." Though I was born in the world of the Whites, I am Comanche. My life with the Numunah is everything, and the mainstay of our life will always be the buffalo. We know this. We eat its meat fresh and also dried. The skins we use for robes and saddles and shelter. We make shields stronger than the white man's bullets. We sew as many as 15 buffalo skins together to make our tipis. The fur is woven into ropes or made into pillows. Even the buffalo's teeth become a rattle for my baby, Quanah.

Some of the things that we got from the Whites were good. Arrowheads made from iron were stronger than stone. Cloth was warm and light and protected us in the winter. Comancheros came from Santa Fe to sell us these goods, and we traded them captives and buffalo robes. But nothing that the Whites did with the buffalo was good.

Though we believed that the buffalo of Texas would be only for Indians, White hunters still came onto the plains. They killed only for the hides, racing to kill the buffalo before other hunters could kill and skin them. We know that unless the hunters are stopped, the buffalo will soon be gone.

For the Numunah, winter used to be a good time. Buffalo were in their prime in the late fall, and we stocked up for winter when their coats were thick and their meat was fat.

With each season it grows harder to find the buffalo. Now, the winter is called, "the time our babies cry for food." And without the buffalo, my people do not know any way to live. We can only starve, or go to the reservations.

The man sitting on the pile of buffalo hides is Charlie Rath, one of the largest buffalo hide dealers on the Plains. He founded Rath City (now gone) near Hamlin as a hide shipping center, and was a partner in the Conrad-Rath Store in Ft. Griffin, a major supplier of guns and ammunition to Texas buffalo hunters.

There's More to the Story

See pages 146–147 for information on these topics:

Commercial Buffalo Hunting

- Where the Buffalo Roam
- The Hunt Begins
- Ready to Harvest
- Many Ways to Profit

During the drought of the 1880s, people shipped their gathered bones from the railroad boneyard, then at the Frontier Texas! site, to bone china, button and fertilizer factories.

CHAPTER 4

Military on the Frontier

Forts housed the military, whose role evolved from peacekeeping to warfare.

For almost fifty years, the U. S. military patrolled the Texas frontier.

The first U. S. military forts were established after the Mexican-American War to prevent the Comanche, now wards of the U. S., from raiding into Mexico.

As more Anglos pushed westward, conflict between Indians and settlers grew. Additional forts were built along ever-westward lines to help control the Indians.

In 1871, an Indian attack on the Warren Wagon Train near present-day Graham, Texas, led to a government change in Indian policy—from peacekeeping to one of containment or eradication.

Fort Phantom Hill

Fort Phantom Hill was established in 1851 to defend settlers, and immigrants headed to California's gold fields, from Indian attack.

Officially called the "Post on the Clear Fork of the Brazos," the fort was one of a second line of forts built on the Texas frontier along a route that had been explored and selected by Captain Randolph B. Marcy.

The fort was home to five companies of the U.S. Fifth Infantry. Life at the isolated fort was difficult, and there was an insufficient supply of water. By 1853 the fort was abandoned, and later set afire.

From 1858 to 1861 the site served as "Way Station Number 54" on the Butterfield Overland Mail stage route. Later, it became a buffalo hide trade town.

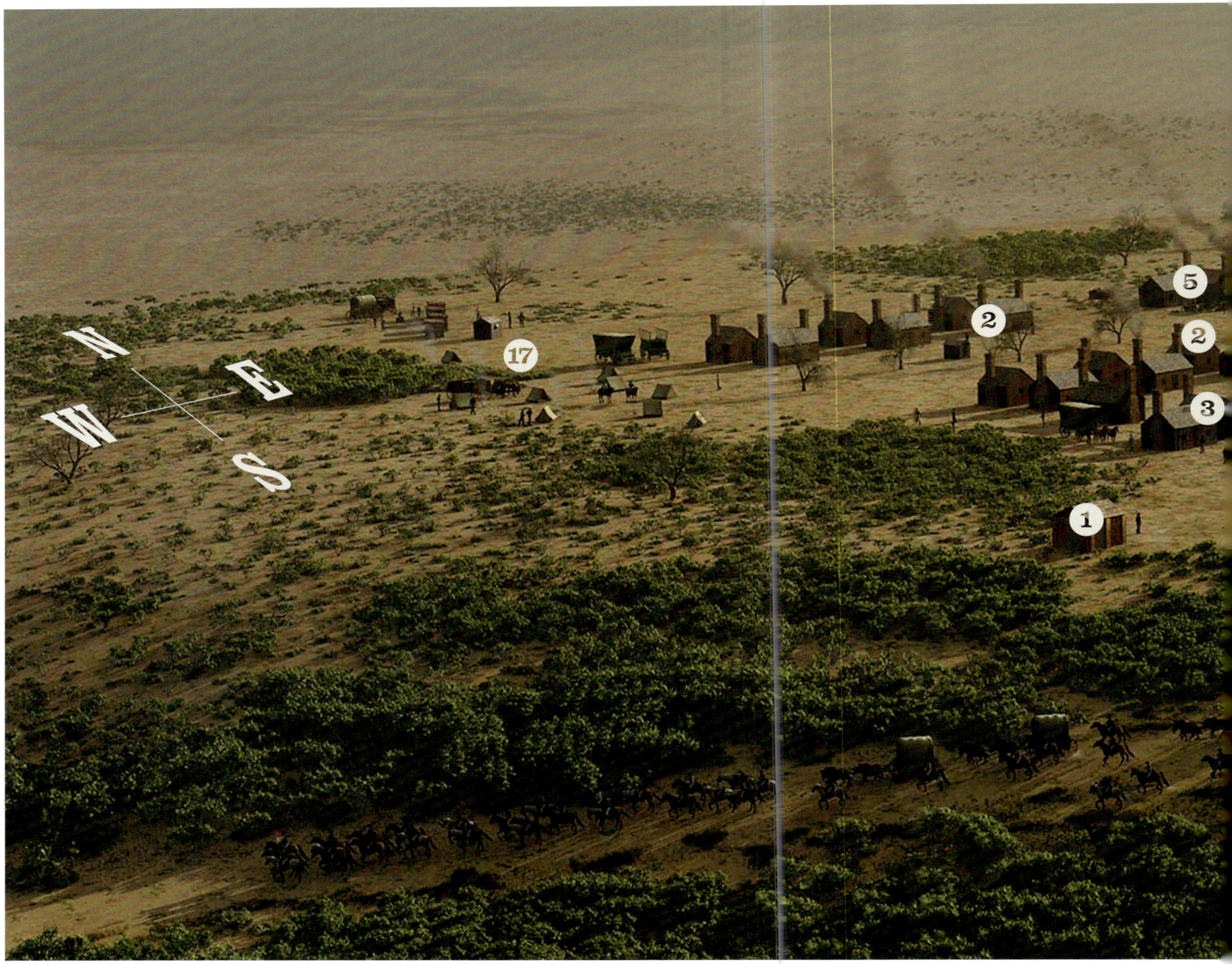

LEGEND:
1. Powder Magazine
2. Officers Row
3. Commanding Officers Quarters
4. Guard House or Jail
5. Blacksmith's Shop and Quarters
6. Commissary
7. Enlisted Barracks and Kitchens
8. Latrines

9. Hospital
10. Surgeon's Quarters
11. Sutler's Store

12. Bake House
13. Laundresses Quarters
14. Stables

15. Horse Corral
16. Mule Corral
17. Sutler's Camps

Illustration for Frontier Texas! by Andy Simmons

U.S. Military Forts in Texas

Several lines of forts were designed to tighten the noose on *Comancheria*.

The First Line of Forts, 1849–1852

Indians had raided into Mexico for a hundred years. To stop the raids, the U. S. government built forts across Texas, and along the Mexican border, to fence in *Comancheria's* side south.

Second Line of Forts, 1852–1861

The military built a second line of forts 150 miles west of the old Comanche frontier to chart routes across the plains for gold-seekers rushing to California.

These new forts were better located geographically to take advantage of timber, water, and terrain features—and to better patrol against Comanche raids. Forts Davis and Bliss further strengthened the overland road to the west and more tightly contained the Comanche.

Post-Civil War Forts

A third line of forts were active after the Civil War. Forts Concho, Griffin, Richardson and Elliot enforced compliance with the Medicine Lodge Treaty of 1867—a treaty in which Indians had agreed to move to reservations in exchange for maintaining rights to hunt buffalo on the Plains.

Waging War Against the Comanche

As Indian violence escalated, the Army adopted the strategy of "total war" that had successfully ended the Civil War in the South.

Generals Phillip Sheridan and William Tecumseh Sherman—both Civil War officers experienced in Total War tactics—directed a relentless pursuit of Indians in Texas—especially during the winter when food supplies were already low.

But it was Colonel Ranald Mackenzie who proved himself one of the most effective military commanders in American history. In 1874 he destroyed large Comanche villages in Palo Duro Canyon. He then ordered the killing of 1000 Comanche horses—crippling the Indians. It was the beginning of the end of Indian resistance.

A year later the famous chief Quanah Parker and 407 starving followers surrendered to Mackenzie at Ft. Sill, Indian Territory.

Mackenzie would later succeed in moving other Western tribes to reservations—the Sioux, the Cheyenne, Utes and the Apache.

TOP LEFT: *Colonel Ronald Mackenzie, Fourth United States Cavalry*

TOP RIGHT: *Lieutenant General Philip Sheridan, Commander of Division of the Missouri*

LOWER LEFT: *General William Sherman, Commander General of the U. S. Army*

Illustration by Charles Schreyvogel (1861–1912)

Soldiering as an Opportunity

The Army provided opportunity for blacks and immigrants.

During the Civil War freed slaves served in the U. S. Army. At its end many were assigned duty in the south to help with Reconstruction. Others were sent to the western frontier. The Indians called them buffalo soldiers because their hair was like the buffalo's. These soldiers served with distinction during the dangerous frontier conflicts.

Many immigrants saw the military as a way to receive a steady paycheck, and to learn English. During the 1850s twice as many immigrants enlisted as did Americans.

Indian scouts, black teamsters and servants were also employed. In 1870 pay for privates was cut from $16 to $13 per month. As a result, one third of the Army's enlisted personnel deserted.

Marching in the Desert with the Buffalo Soldiers *Painting by Frederick Remington*

"The duty of repressing hostilities among Indian tribes, and of protecting frontier settlements from their depredations, is the most difficult one which the Army has now to perform; and nowhere has it been found more difficult than on the Western frontier of Texas."

—Jefferson Davis, U. S. Secretary of War

Buffalo Soldiers at Fort Concho

Established in 1867, Fort Concho was one of the most important frontier forts in the post-Civil War period.

Fort Concho was headquarters for the 10th Cavalry, which consisted of African-American troops. The Plains Indians called them "buffalo soldiers"—a name that the black soldiers carried with pride.

Most of their duties included routine patrols and escorts, but they served their country well in campaigns against the Comanche and Kiowa.

The fort was located in San Angelo, 90 miles southwest of Abilene. A significant complex of the 40 original limestone buildings remains at the fort site today.

Texas Rangers and the Colt Revolver

TOP: *The "Walker" Colt Revolver Six shot, .44-caliber, percussion revolver used by the Texas Rangers.*

BELOW: *Colonel Walker of the Texas Rangers—designer of the Walker Colt.*

While a Republic, Texans formed their own militia—the Texas Rangers.

Following the Civil War, the Rangers aggressively fought the Indians.

The Comanche referred to Texans as ‘those who follow us home" because the Texas settlers and Rangers aggressively pursued raiding Indians. It was dangerous work, and some estimate the Rangers suffered 50% casualties.

Rangers like Jack Hays, Samuel Walker, and Ben McColluch became skilled Indian fighters and helped develop the repeating pistol to use against Indians.

The Comanche's bows and arrows provided superior firepower to single-shot weapons, but were no match for the repeating revolver, which revolutionized plains warfare.

"When a Ranger wanted to arrest a man his first action was to draw his six-shooter and 'get the drop' on his prospective prisoner. No matter how desperate a man might be, he would not take the chances of resisting arrest when he was locking into the muzzle of a loaded revolver with a Ranger's finger playing nervously around the trigger thereof."

—N. A. Jennings,
Texas Ranger

"My rattlesnake, my only pet, is dead. He grew sick and would not eat his frogs and died one night."

—Lieutenant Colonel Robert E. Lee
in letters to home from the Texas frontier

"The attack was a surprise. The Indians were generally in their wigwams. No fire was made by the Indians until they were fired upon and some of them killed. They showed no disposition to fight. The women were screaming about the camp, some of them in plain English declaring they were friendly. Captain Fosset declined to communicate with them, saying that he recognized no friendly Indians on the Texas frontier."

—Brigadier General J. D. McAdoo, Texas State Troops,
Confederate States of America

Frontier Firepower

Firepower was a life and death issue on the frontier.

The Indian's ability to fire rapidly and accurately with their handmade bows gave them superiority over their opponents who were armed with single-shot weapons. The Texas Rangers influenced the adaptation of repeating arms for use in the intimacy of frontier conflicts. When reliable six-shooters became available, firepower superiority shifted against the Indians.

LEFT *Warriors could shoot an arrow every few seconds with deadly accuracy. In the close-range conflicts of the frontier, single-shot guns were no match.*

NEXT PAGE, LEFT TO RIGHT: *1805 Harpers Ferry Pistol Single Shot, .58-caliber, flintlock pistol*

Colt "Texas Patterson" Revolver: Five shot, .36-caliber percussion revolver without loading lever

The "Walker" Colt Revolver Six shot, .44-caliber, percussion revolver used by the Texas Rangers.

Colt Cattleman Single Action Revolver: Six shot, .45-caliber cartridge revolver

Jack Hayes of the Texas Rangers

"Me and Red Wing not afraid to go to hell together. Captain Jack heap brave; not afraid to go to hell by himself."

—Chief Flacco, Lipan Apache guide [regarding John (Jack) Coffee Hays]

Marcy is portrayed by Garrett Schenck, who has appeared in many commercials and industrial productions as well as TV series such as Walker, Texas Ranger *and* Dallas. *His movies include* Necessary Roughness *and* Frequent Flyer.

Spirit Guide

Randolph Marcy

A career Army officer born in Massachusetts in 1812, Randolph Marcy explored the Southwest in the 1840s and 1850s for the Army on mapping and research expeditions. He plotted a trail from Fort Smith, Arkansas, to Santa Fe, and in 1851 he assisted in selecting sites for the forts that would later protect the frontier. His writings were some of the first recorded information on travel through the West.

Question #1: What brought you to Texas?

I was assigned to Texas in 1846 during the war with Mexico, and I fought in the battles of Palo Alto and Resaca de la Palma. Then the Army sent me to this area to search for natural roads, water and timber. On these journeys across the Texas plains, we discovered the source of the Red River and mapped the first trail for settlers moving further West. I guess I did all right, because that route is now called Marcy's Trail, and it is the route followed by many going to the California Gold Rush in '49, as well as the Butterfield Stage and the Goodnight-Loving Trail.

Question #2: What was the original role of the military on the frontier?

When the military first came to the Texas frontier, our mission was simply to monitor activities by all parties—Indians, settlers and traders—without getting directly involved. In 1851 I participated in establishing a line of forts on the frontier, including Fort Phantom, just a few miles from here. It was a strange time for the military. We were under strict orders, in the beginning, to not interfere at all. More than once, our patrols passed Indian bands with white captives crying and pleading for the soldiers to rescue them. Our men did some crying to, but they still weren't allowed to interfere. After the Civil War, that policy changed.

Question #3: What did you think of the Indians you encountered?

Much of our success was due to the help of scouts like Jim Ned and Black Beaver, who were Delaware Indians. We also met on friendly terms with many Comanche leaders, including Buffalo Hump and Sanaco, leader of a Comanche tribe called the Penateka, or "the honey eaters." Later Sanaco decided to fight us and eventually government soldiers killed him up on the Pease River.

Question #4: What kind of men served on the frontier?

Officers were generally well-educated men. The enlisted men came from all walks of life. We had a lot of men fresh off the boats from Ireland and Germany. To them the military was a way to learn the language and start a new life in America. After the Civil War, we had black troops, called buffalo soldiers by the Indians, because of their curly hair and they were tough like the buffalo.

Question #5: What happened here after the Civil War?

After the Civil War, the army became the enforcer of national policy, and our job was to incorporate this area into the nation. Because settlers had moved well beyond our original forts, we built a new line of forts, which included Ft. Richardson, Ft. Griffin and Ft. Concho. Our mission was to

(continued on next page)

enforce Indian treaties, keep things safe for settlers and encourage commerce. To do that we ended up having to fight Indians who defied the national will.

Question #6: How were the Indians defeated?

A common misconception is that the government had thousands of soldiers fighting the Indians, but the truth was that we were small groups out on patrol, a long ways from our posts and our supplies. To keep the troops and animals fed and the men equipped with ammunition, we established smaller outposts where the duty was both boring and dangerous. Battles with the Indians were usually short, intense and at very close range. In the long run, the Indians were defeated by a combination of tactics. To reduce their mobility, we were forced to drive away or kill their horses. That, combined with removing their food supply by slaughtering the buffalo, made it impossible for them to carry on as they always had.

There's More to the Story

See pages 148–155 for information on these topics:

Conflict

- Government Policy
- Quanah Parker
- Controlling the Tribes
- Tough Attitudes

Frontier Forts

- Securing the Frontier
- Additional Fortifications
- The Post War Years
- Peace and Prosperity

Troopers of the Plains

- Doughboys and Pony Soldiers
- A Brittle Sword
- Dawn to Dusk
- Life at the Top

Buffalo Soldiers

- Fighting for Freedom
- Black Men in Army Blue
- Fighting Prejudice with Conduct
- The Tools of the Soldier

Cowboys and Longhorns

Here's why the great Texas cattle drives took place.

CHAPTER 5

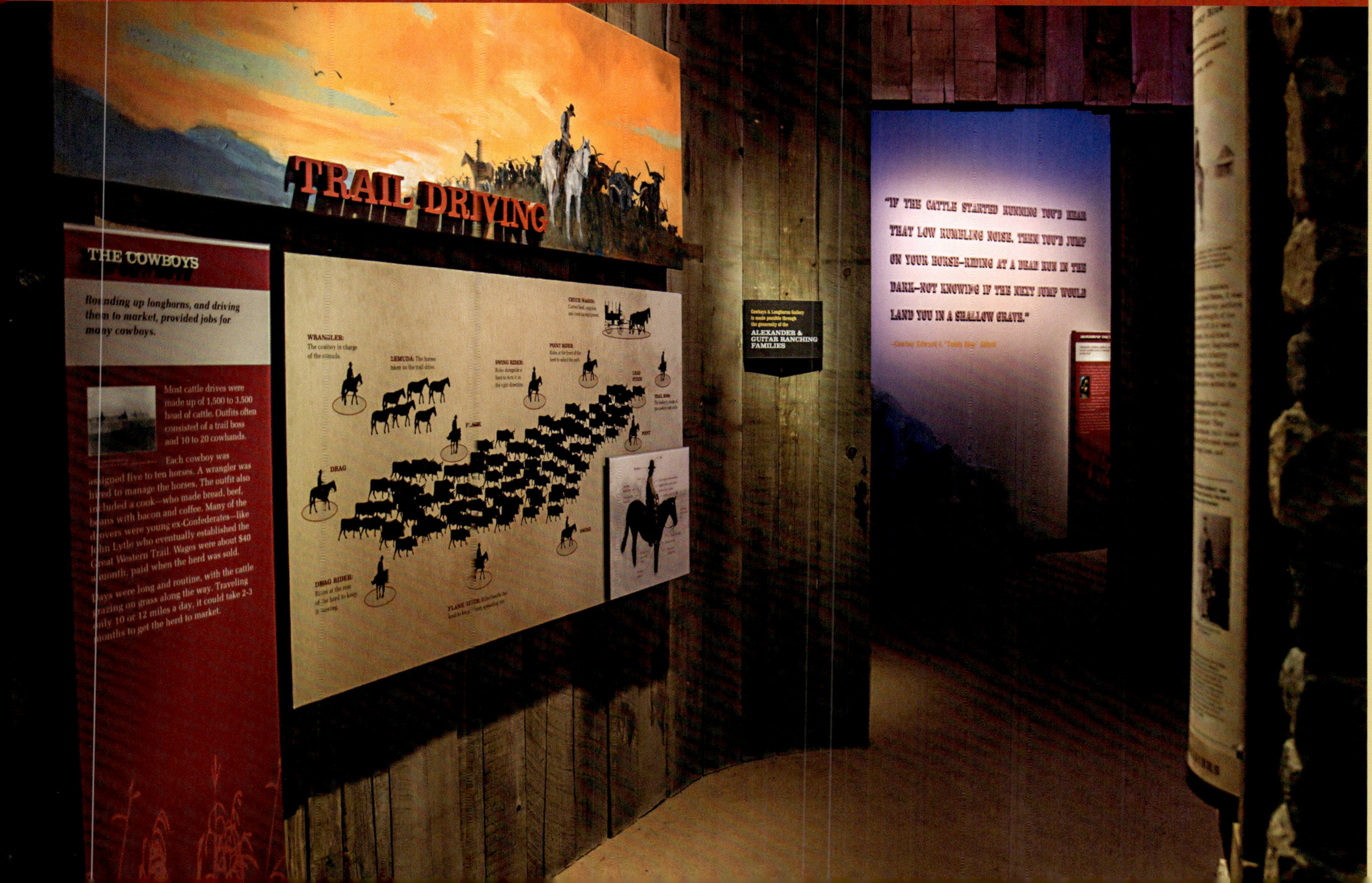

By the end of the Civil War millions of wild longhorns, mostly unclaimed, roamed Texas.

Texans began to drive the longhorns across open range and the Indian Territory to railheads in Kansas for shipment to eastern markets.

Hundreds of herds of cattle were driven up trails to the existing railheads, as a Texas steer worth $3 could be sold at a railhead for $30.

Cowboys were paid well for the hard, dangerous trip—and herd owners often amassed fortunes. In less than 25 years, cowboys drove millions of cattle out of Texas over the cattle trails.

MURAL NOTES

A Long, Lonesome Trail

Original Artwork by H. C. Zachry

"John Lytle, who had his open range ranch near Abilene (and for whom Lytle Lake is named) helped open the largest of the longhorn cattle trails, the Western Trail. It was slow work to herd the wild longhorns from south or central Texas across the Red River and the Indian Territory (now Oklahoma), with the boredom periodically shattered by the terror of Indian encounters, stampedes, rustlers and animal-related accidents. The sunset in the mural symbolizes the coming end of the trail drives and the vastness of the sky and land is to convey just how much these cowboys and trail drivers were on their own, in the middle of nowhere, without backup."

—H. C. Zachry

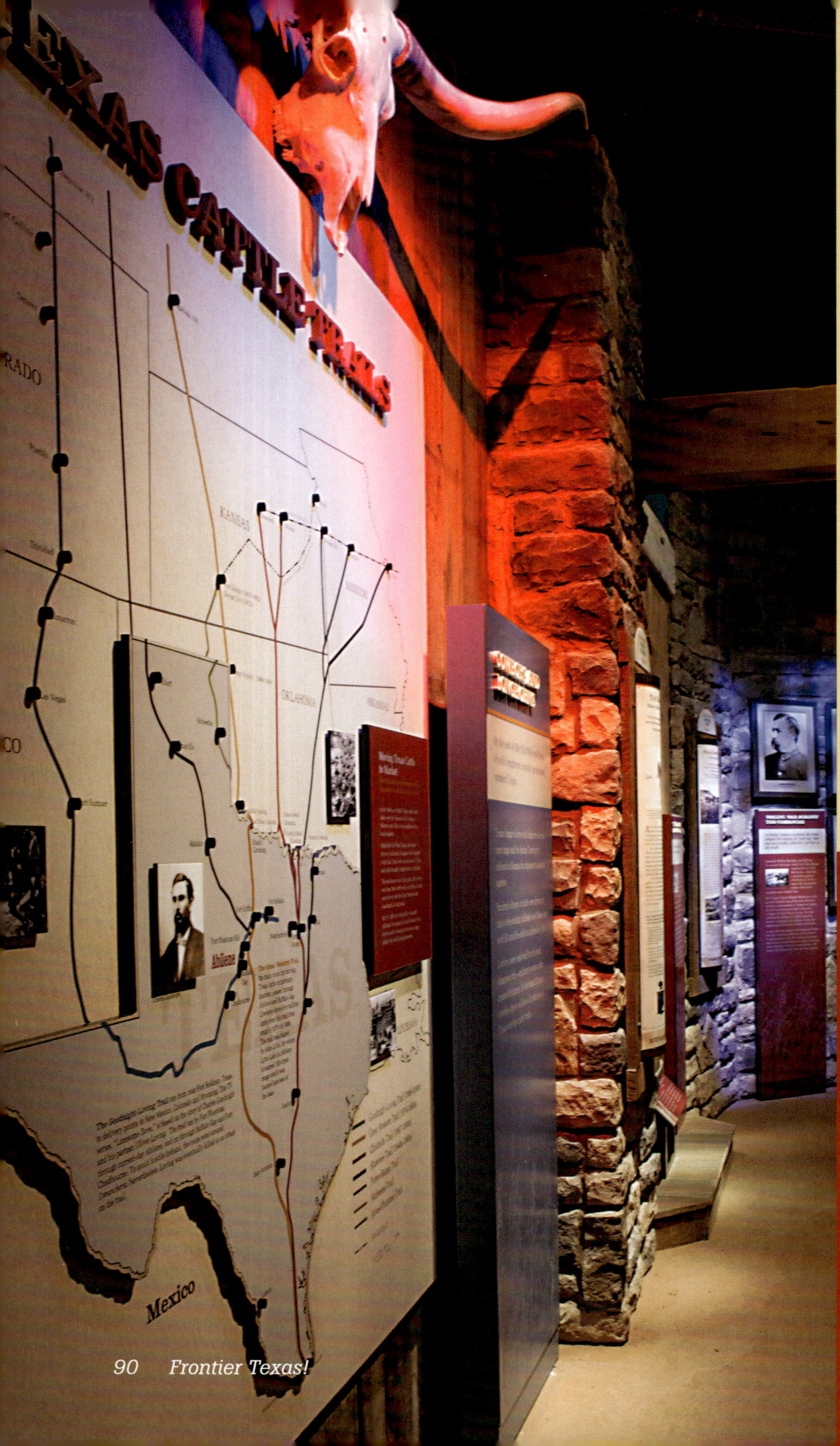

Moving Texas Cattle to Market

Cattle trails were the primary means of moving Texas cattle to market in the late 19th century.

In the 1840s and 1850s Texas cattle were taken over the Shawnee trail to Iowa, Missouri and Ohio to be slaughtered for local markets.

During the Civil War, Texas cattle were driven to railheads in Kansas to be shipped to the East. There were no railroads in Texas, and cattle brought a higher price in the East.

The best-known era of the great cattle drives was from 1866–1890, when millions of cattle were driven over the Great Western and Goodnight Loving trails.

But by 1890, the availability of nearby railroads, the spread of cattle disease (tick fever) and the fencing of the open range ended the trail driving business.

> "The year of 1877, we started a herd to Kansas. I routed right through Buffalo Gap, where Carter and Grounds had a little supply store and that was the whole town at the time. From there we went on by where the present town of Abilene is located, but then that also was a bald prairie."
>
> —Bob Lauderdale, Texas cowboy

TEXAS CATTLE TRAILS

The Great Western Trail

The Great Western Trail, the main route for moving Texas cattle to northern markets, passed through Abilene and Buffalo Gap. Cowboys drove five million cattle over this trail from roughly 1874 to 1886. The trail was blazed by John Lytle, for whom Lytle Lake in Abilene is named. His open range ranch was located just east of the lake.

The Goodnight-Loving Trail

The Goodnight-Loving Trail ran from near Graham, Texas, to railheads in New Mexico, Colorado and Wyoming. The TV series, "Lonesome Dove," is based on the story of Charles Goodnight and his partner, Oliver Loving. The trail ran by Fort Phantom, through current-day Abilene, and on through Buffalo Gap and Fort Chadbourne. To avoid hostile Indians, the route went around *Comancheria*. Nevertheless, Loving was eventually killed in an attack on the trail.

Reynolds is portrayed by Robert Lott, who has had film roles in Varsity Blues, The Only Thrill, No Small Ways *and* The Life of David Gale. *His television work includes* Two For Texas, A Face To Kill For *and* Walker, Texas Ranger.

Spirit Guide

George Reynolds

Born in Alabama in 1844, George Reynolds and his family soon moved to East Texas where they farmed for 12 years before moving west, eventually settling on the Brazos in Stephens County. At 15, George was riding pony express-type mail deliveries through hostile Indian territory and later fought with the Confederate Army during the Civil War. After the war, he and two other men drove a herd of cattle to New Mexico, reportedly the first herd over what would become the Goodnight-Loving Trail. While fighting Indians in 1867, he took an arrow in the stomach and lived with the arrowhead in his body until it was surgically removed 16 years later. He married into the Matthews family in 1867, and established ranching operations throughout West Texas and drove cattle through the western states and Canada. At his death in 1925, the Reynolds Cattle Company owned several hundred thousand acres of ranchland across West Texas and the Panhandle.

I tell you what—there was nothing worse than a night stampede, and we all went through it one time or another. When a big lightning storm rolled in on your herd at night, you could see the electricity glowing green on the cattle's horns and the horse's ears.

When the cattle get nervous, anything can set 'em running—charging blind across the prairie so's all you can do is try to ride faster—hope your horse doesn't trip in a prairie dog hole. You're riding hell for leather and the only thing you can see is the sparks from your horse's hooves striking rocks.

If you're lucky, you get in front and turn the leaders back into the herd, so that they all begin to slow down and mill.

A whole night of that and you're so tired you can hardly sit a saddle, but come first light you start heading 'em back to the trail, just hoping all your friends are still alive and that you haven't lost a lot of cattle.

After the Civil War, with no money on the frontier but lots of cattle, I took two men from the Clear Fork country and we drove a herd 600 miles to Fort Sumner in New Mexico. Because of Indian danger and a lack of water, we skirted around the Comancheria by following the old Butterfield Stage Road across the Texas prairie to the Pecos River and into New Mexico. My friends Charles Goodnight and Oliver Loving later made this route famous with their drives. In fact, I was on the cattle drive with those boys when the Indians killed Mr. Loving. My brother helped Charlie and Bose Ikard bring his body back to Weatherford to be buried.

Indians, weather, stampedes . . . it was dangerous work. Cattle worth $3 around here were worth ten times that in New Mexico or Kansas, but trail driving was a tough job.

Our goal was to get the cattle to market, collect the money and get back home without getting robbed or killed.

I was young . . . 25, maybe . . . but many of the cowboys weren't even 18 years old. They made $40 a month for their hard work and the risks they took. That kind of money could stake you to a new life, here on the frontier.

Outlaws and Indians were a danger wherever you went. Families in the region sometimes had to fort up for mutual protection. In one fight with Comanches on the Double Mountain Fork of the Brazos, I was shot in the belly with an arrow. One of my pals killed and scalped the warrior that got me.

That arrow was stuck in me so hard that my brothers broke the shaft off trying to pull it out. It looked like I would die, but I didn't. About 15 years later, I was in Kansas City and a surgeon cut that steel arrow point out of me. In fact, I still have the arrowhead (holds up watch chain with arrowhead). Sure feels better on the outside of my belly than on the inside.

"Oh bury me not on the lone prairie.
These words came slow and mournfully
From the bleedin' lips of the youth who lay
On his dyin' bed at the close of day.

Oh bury me not on the lone prairie
Where the wild coyotes howl over me,
In a narrow grave, just six by three.
Oh, bury me not on the lone prairie.

I've always wished to be laid when I died
In a little churchyard on the green hillside;
By my mama's grave please let mine be,
And bury me not on the lone prairie.

Oh, bury me not . . . and his voice stopped there.
But we took no heed of his dyin' prayer;
In a narrow grave, just six by three . . .
We buried him there, on the lone prairie."

—*Bury Me Not on the Lone Prairie,*
traditional cowboy tune, author unknown.

Trail Driving

The dangers of the trail were many.

Stampedes, Indians, outlaws, and severe weather were a constant threat on the trail.

The wild longhorns would stampede at a loud clap of thunder. Some of the cattle would be trampled and the herd scattered. Cowboys, riding full speed, would try to make the herd run in a circle to tire them out. Riding at a full run through the night, in rain, on uneven ground, could lead to serious injuries or death.

Other dangers included attacks by Indians or outlaws, and the risk of infection from cuts and wounds. Home remedies were the only medicine available.

Crossing flooded rivers presented another danger, as the cowboys had to make the herds swim into the swollen streams and then follow them. Panicked cattle, frightened horses, and swirling water made a very risky, and sometimes deadly, combination.

MURAL NOTES

Stampede!

Original Art by H. C. Zachry

"One of the most horrific events on the cattle trail, as well as one of the most frequent, was the stampede. A clap of thunder, a wolf's howl, a bucking horse—any number of things could make the longhorns bolt from their bed ground and tear away in panic at full speed. When stampedes happened, the cowboys rode hell for leather to try to reach the front of the herd, in order to gradually turn the leaders into a circle and slow the herd down. Riding full speed in the pitch dark night over the brush, gulleys, rocks and holes of the prairie—knowing that an encounter with any of them could mean broken bones or being trampled to death—must have been terrifying. I let a flash of lightening briefly illuminate our scene so that we could see a bit of the inky blackness of the unknown."

—H. C. Zachry

"If the cattle started running you'd hear that low rumbling noise. Then you'd jump on your horse riding at a dead run in the dark, not knowing if the next jump would land you in a shallow grave."

—Edward C. "Teddy Blue" Abbott, cowboy

"It's just what I've been wanting to do all my life . . . I've wanted to live on the frontier—be a part of it. I'm not worried about dangers—Indians or whatever else might be out there."

—John Williams, pioneer

RIGHT: *George Reynolds, trail driver, comes to life through spectral imagery.*

"They kept their places around a herd and under all circumstances; and if they had to fight they were always ready. Timid men were not known among them—the life did not fit them."

—Charles Goodnight, Texas rancher (about his cowboys)

Stampeding longhorns in Frontier Texas!

There's More to the Story

See pages 156–157 for information on these topics:

Trail Drivers and Longhorns

- Hide and Horn
- The Men Who Led the Way
- Where They Went
- The Great Roundup

"Served with me four years on Goodnight-Loving trail, never shirked or disobeyed an order, rode with me in many stampedes, participated in three engagements with Comanche. Splendid behavior."

—epitaph on the headstone of Bose Ikard, a black cowboy, composed by his friend and employer, Charles Goodnight

Frontier Settlements

People, both good and bad, created the frontier towns that became legendary in western books and movies.

As more soldiers, trail drivers, buffalo hunters and other pioneers came into the area, ramshackle settlements grew up on the frontier.

Some settlements grew up around the frontier forts, while others developed as trading posts where buffalo hunters could sell hides and resupply their crews.

These frontier outposts attracted everyone looking to make a buck—including legitimate businesspeople, gamblers, camp followers, prostitutes and other rough characters.

"At the time, the name of Texas, more especially West Texas, was a synonym for lawlessness, desperadoes, and all that was wild and bad. There was also a leaven of good, those rugged self-disciplined pioneers, men and women of foresight and courage, who were willing to brave the dangerous unknown and undergo countless hardships and privations for the sake of widening their horizons and preparing an easier road for their children."

—Sallie Reynolds Matthews, pioneer

Initially the towns were unorganized and dangerous—wild and wooly places where life was cheap.

Survival was the order of the day in the ramshackle towns and trading posts that sprung up in areas already made hostile by the mix of cultures, professions and personalities. Indian raids sometimes occurred near, or even in the settlements. It was a time of life and death struggles.

Living on the lawless frontier often gave people a calloused view of legality, equality and fairness. When their relevant economics faded, many of these towns settled back into the dust from which they had risen.

RIGHT: *Indians resisted the invasion of their territory—and savagely attacked the settlers, who reciprocated with vengeance. These scalps on the shield at Frontier Texas! were taken by Indians from girls or women killed east of Abilene's present site in the early 1870s. The next page tells their tragic story. These rare artifacts are shown through the courtesy of Cecil W. Brown.*

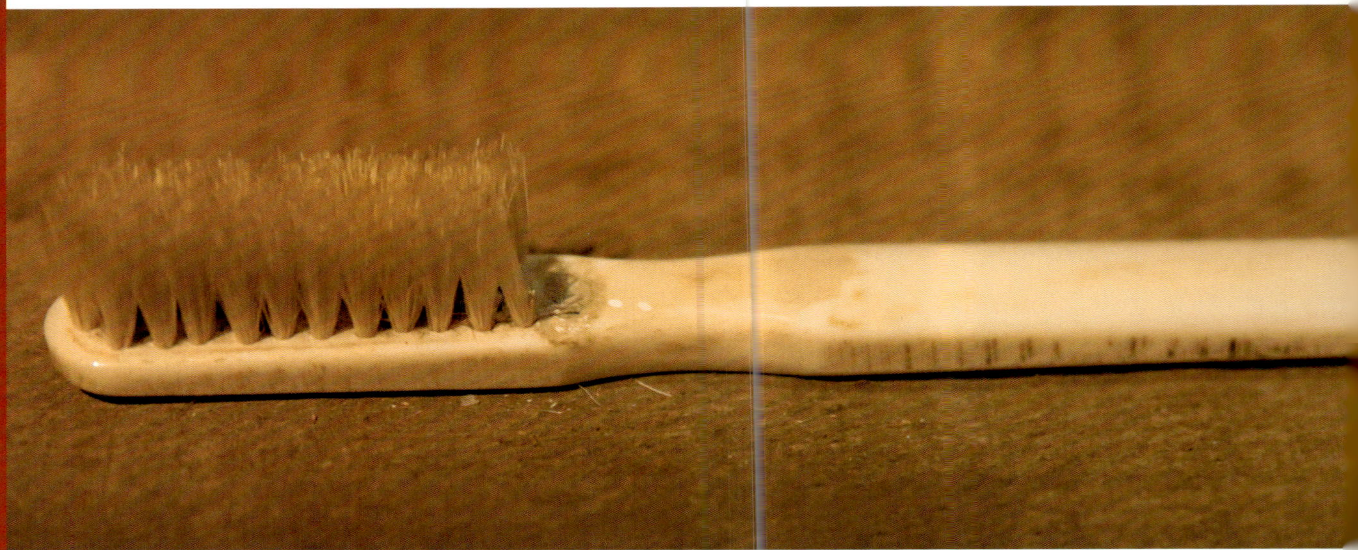

Community toothbrushes (like this example from Frontier Texas!) were often hung outside stage stops and boarding houses, for free use by all.

"The Indians got so bad that the boys carried guns to and from school. It was not unusual for an Indian to jump up from a bush or from behind a tree and shoot an arrow into someone."

—Julia Thompson Neal, pioneer

"After a man has served a few years on the frontiers he becomes wary, suspicious of danger and watchful of its approach, until these become characteristics of his everyday life."

—George F. Price, settler

Why is That Dead Horse Tied to a Hole in the Ground?

To carry a dead Indian chief to his glory.

Many strange stories came from the Texas frontier, where anyone and everyone faced the risk of being cast into eternity in the blink of an eye.

In 1872 before towns were established in this area, two teenagers were traveling by wagon to another ranch. As they stopped for the night, a cowboy joined their camp. He was helping unhitch their mules when 30 Indians suddenly attacked.

Chaos followed as guns exploded and arrows flew. Indians were yelling and mules plunging about. Men screamed as they were hit with bullets and arrows. An arrow pierced the cowboy—the feathers sticking out in front and the arrowhead in back. The boys were also wounded.

A fatal mistake is made.

The Indian chief—mistakenly thinking the boys were out of ammunition—leapt off his horse, held up his war shield and ran toward the three men with his tomahawk.

One of the boys aimed under the chief's shield and shot him. The chief staggered about, singing his death song, as the other warriors crowded around. Using the distraction, the boys and the cowboy jumped on the mules and escaped.

The cowboy's mule had been wounded and soon fell dead. He urged the others to ride on, saying, "Save yourselves, this arrow will kill me anyway."

The boys dashed through the darkness to a nearby ranch, gathered reinforcements and rode back to the battleground. Surprisingly, the cowboy was still alive. He eventually lived, in fact, to quite an old age.

They see a very strange sight.

At the battleground, they saw a puzzling sight. Lying on the ground was a dead Indian horse. Around the horse's neck was a rope that led into a freshly dug grave. When the men unearthed the grave, they found the dead Indian chief—one hand holding the horse's rope, and the other hand holding his war shield.

Death on the frontier.

On the war shield were scalps of three women the chief had killed and scalped—one grey-haired, one black, and one red-headed.

On the shield shown on the previous page are the same scalps that were buried with the chief almost 150 years ago.

MURAL NOTES

Journey into Eternity

Original Art by H. C. Zachry

"I think this is my favorite mural. The true story it represents is so powerful. I considered a number of different story moments while deciding what to illustrate, finally settling on this one dramatic moment. To me, this story symbolizes the end of a really powerful culture—and shows the tenacity, the perseverance, the I'm-going-to-survive-no-matter-what attitude of the new culture flooding across the country. On this night, everyone in the story was being stalked by the Pale Rider, and it is a surprise to learn which ones he snatched into eternity."

—H. C. Zachry

Elizabeth Clifton is portrayed by Kit Gwin, who has performed on stage and has appeared in a number of movies, including Graduation Day *and* Dr. T and the Women, *as well as TV shows such as* Walker, Texas Ranger.

Spirit Guide

Elizabeth Carter Clifton

Born in Alabama in 1825, Elizabeth Carter Clifton married a free black in 1842. They came to Texas and established a ranch and the Carter Trading House, a boarding house near Fort Belknap. In 1857, her father-in-law and husband were both murdered. She later married an Army lieutenant, who disappeared eight months later. Her boarding house prospered once the Butterfield Overland Mail began stopping at Fort Belknap. She married one of her ranch hands, who was murdered 18 months later. In 1864, she was captured in the Elm Creek Raid, along with two granddaughters. She was rescued in 1865 and ended up in Fort Griffin with her granddaughter Lottie, where she would lose yet another husband.

Don't think your staring's gonna bother me. If you're looking for a room, I'm all full up. But if you're looking for dinner, I got stew on the stove and plates for twenty.

Running a boarding house sounds like a lot of work, don't it? I'll tell you though, this is easy compared to my first years on the frontier. I come here from Alabama when I was 16. Me and my new husband—he weren't white—came to this raw old Texas frontier. We were way out by ourselves and travelers got to stopping by for a meal or to spend the night. Spite I couldn't read or write, we started the Carter Trading House. We prospered. In fact, we done real good. Started a ranch.

Then one night, a man shot my husband. Murdered him. Killed my father in law, too, while he was at it. Course no lawman came to try to catch the outlaw. It would have been a 100-mile ride and nobody cared enough to do that.

My goodness, times was hard then. There were just a few families scattered in that wilderness between the Clear Fork and the Brazos. We mostly lived in dugouts, just holes in the ground, and sometimes picket houses with dirt floors. When the men folk were away, women and children were left alone and it was up to us to protect ourselves against the Indians and outlaws. I remarried to a military man, a lieutenant. He went out to check on our horses one day and never came back. I suppose Indians or outlaws got him. One was bad as the other. No, white outlaws was worse, cause you couldn't tell they was bad by looking.

The Butterfield Stage started coming by my place, and I done real good off that trade. Married again, too. An Irish cowboy. What a funny man. But a feller killed him too, right out in our pasture.

I guess the worst thing that happened to me was being captured by the Indians. They was mostly Kiowas led by a fellow named Sunboy, came on a big raid. They killed my daughter, Susanna, and her baby boy. Took me and my thirteen year old boy and my two granddaughters, Lottie and Milly. Drug us off through the brush. My boy was sick, couldn't keep up, so they killed him before we barely got started. Poor Milly was just a little girl, she starved to death the first winter in the Indian camps. Lottie and me hung on. They branded Lottie—marked up a circle right on her forehead. It was a fight every day to stay alive. Then, wonders never cease, some troopers traded for us while the band was up in Kansas. From there, in order to get home, I hired out to drive a mule team to Texas. Took two months to make that trip, but Lottie and me was finally back home after two horrible years.

Lottie grew up and married the sheriff at Fort Griffin. They moved up to Tascosa, up in the Panhandle, where he was sheriff. It was a rough place. Lottie died there, poor thing, just 26 years old. I never knew what killed her. Then I hooked up with an old buffalo hunter, and that marriage lasted 11 years fore he died. From there on it's just me, pretty much living hand to mouth, helping run this boarding house in Griffin. I'm not a complainer but if I'd known what 50 years on the Texas frontier would really be like, I might've just stayed in Alabama!

I got to get back to work now. Maybe I'll see you come suppertime.

No. 1] [Sep. 16th, 1858.

OVERLAND MAIL COMPANY.

THROUGH TIME SCHEDULE BETWEEN

ST. LOUIS, MO., MEMPHIS, TENN. } & SAN FRANCISCO, CAL.

GOING WEST.

LEAVE.	DAYS.	Hour.	Distance, Place to Place.	Time allowed.	Av'ge Miles per Hour.
			Miles.	No. Hours	
St. Louis, Mo., & Memphis, Tenn.	Every Monday & Thursday,	8.00 A.M			
P. R. R. Terminus, "	" Monday & Thursday,	6.00 P.M	160	10	16
Springfield, "	" Wednesday & Saturday	7.45 A.M	143	37¾	3¾
Fayetteville, "	" Thursday & Sunday,	10.15 A.M	100	26¼	3¾
Fort Smith, Ark.	" Friday & Monday,	3.30 A.M	65	17¼	3¾
Sherman, Texas	" Sunday & Wednesday,	12.30 A.M	205	45	4½
Fort Belknap, "	" Monday & Thursday,	9.00 A.M	146½	32½	4½
Fort Chadbourn, "	" Tuesday & Friday,	3.15 P.M	136	30¼	4½
Pecos River, (Em. Crossing)	" Thursday & Sunday,	3.45 A.M	165	36½	4½
El Paso,	" Saturday & Tuesday,	11.00 A.M	248½	55¼	4½
Soldier's Farewell	" Sunday & Wednesday,	8.30 P.M	150	33½	4½
Tucson, Arizona	" Tuesday & Friday,	1.30 P.M	184½	41	4½
Gila River,* "	" Wednesday & Saturday	9.00 P.M	141	31½	4½
Fort Yuma, Cal.	" Friday & Monday,	3.00 A.M	135	30	4½
San Bernardino "	" Saturday & Tuesday,	11.00 P.M	200	44	4½
Ft. Tejon, (Via Los Angeles)	" Monday & Thursday,	7.30 A.M	150	32½	4½
Visalia, "	" Tuesday & Friday,	11.30 A.M	127	28	4½
Firebaugh's Ferry, "	" Wednesday & Saturday	5.30 A.M	82	18	4½
(Arrive) San Francisco,	" Thursday & Sunday,	8.30 A.M	163	27	6

GOING EAST.

LEAVE.	DAYS.	Hour.	Distance, Place to Place.	Time allowed.	Av'ge Miles per Hour.
			Miles.	No. Hours	
San Francisco, Cal.	Every Monday & Thursday,	8.00 A.M			
Firebaugh's Ferry, "	" Tuesday & Friday,	11.00 A.M	163	27	6
Visalia, "	" Wednesday & Saturday,	5.00 A.M	82	18	4½
Ft. Tejon, (Via Los Angeles)	" Thursday & Sunday,	9.00 A.M	127	28	4½
San Bernardino, "	" Friday & Monday,	5.30 P.M	150	32½	4½
Fort Yuma, "	" Sunday & Wednesday,	1.30 P.M	200	44	4½
Gila River,* Arizona	" Monday & Thursday,	7.30 P.M	135	30	4½
Tucson, "	" Wednesday & Saturday	3.00 A.M	141	31½	4½
Soldier's Farewell,	" Thursday & Sunday,	8.00 P.M	184½	41	4½
El Paso, Tex.	" Saturday & Tuesday,	5.30 A.M	150	33½	4½
Pecos River, (Em. Crossing)	" Monday & Thursday	12.45 P.M	248½	55¼	4½
Fort Chadbourn, "	" Wednesday & Saturday	1.15 A.M	165	36½	4½
Fort Belknap, "	" Thursday & Sunday,	7.30 A.M	136	30¼	4½
Sherman, "	" Friday & Monday,	4.00 P.M	146½	32½	4½
Fort Smith, Ark.	" Sunday & Wednesday,	1.00 P.M	205	45	4½
Fayetteville, Mo.	" Monday, & Thursday,	6.15 A.M	65	17¼	3¾
Springfield, "	" Tuesday & Friday,	8.45 A.M	100	26¼	3¾
P. R. R. Terminus, "	" Wednesday & Saturday	10.30 P.M	143	37¾	3¾
(Arrive) St. Louis, Mo., & Memphis, Tenn.	" Thursday & Sunday,		160	10	16

This Schedule may not be exact—Superintendents, Agents, Station-men, Conductors, Drivers and all employees are particularly directed to use every possible exertion to get the Stages through in quick time, even though they may be ahead of this time.

If they are behind this time, it will be necessary to urge the animals on to the highest speed that they can be driven without injury.

Remember that no allowance is made in the time for ferries, changing teams, &c. It is therefore necessary that each driver increase his speed over the average per hour enough to gain the necessary time for meals, changing teams, crossing ferries, &c.

Every person in the Company's employ will always bear in mind that each minute of time is of importance. If each driver on the route loses fifteen (15) minutes, it would make a total loss of time, on the entire route, of twenty-five (25) hours, or, more than one day. If each one loses ten (10) minutes it would make a total loss of sixteen and one half (16½) hours, or, the best part of a day.

On the contrary, if each driver gains that amount of time, it leaves a margin of time against accidents and extra delays.

All hands will see the great necessity of promptness and dispatch: every minute of time is valuable as the Company are under heavy forfeit if the mail is behind time.

Conductors must note the hour and date of departure from Stations, the causes of delay, if any, and all particulars. They must also report the same fully to their respective Superintendents.

JOHN BUTTERFIELD.
Pres't.

* The Station referred to on Gila River, is [illegible] miles west of Maricopa Wells.

TOP: *Overland Mail Schedule*
BOTTOM: *Stagecoach in Texas*
RIGHT: *Stage Coach Sketch*

Butterfield Overland Stage

The Butterfield Overland Stage operated from 1857 to 1861, carrying passengers and mail from Missouri to California.

It took 25 days to make the entire trip on the Butterfield Overland Stage, the fastest route west. A third of the trip was spent crossing Texas.

The stage ran through forts Richardson, Belknap, Phantom Hill, passed through Buffalo Gap and on to Fort Chadbourne, then across the plains between the Concho and Pecos Rivers and through the Guadalupe Pass to El Paso and points west.

"Had I not just come out over the route, I would be perfectly willing to go back, but I now know what Hell is like. I've just had 24 days of it."

—Waterman Ormsby, *New York Herald* newspaper

Johnson is portrayed by C. Anthony Jackson, who has appeared in Walker, Texas Ranger, The Big Story *and* Midnight, *as well as many TV commercials and industrial films.*

Spirit Guide

Britt Johnson

Born a slave in Tennessee in 1840, Britt Johnson came to Texas with his master, Moses Johnson. As a reward for his loyalty and hard work, Britt was appointed foreman of a ranch in Young County and had his own horses and cattle. In 1864 during the Elm Creek Raid, Indians killed Britt's son and took his wife and two daughters captive. His attempts to find his family became the source of legend. In 1865, he was able to secure their freedom and the family returned to Texas. He used his renown to build a business as a freighter between Weatherford and Fort Griffin. He died heroically in 1871 defending a wagon train he was leading through Young County when it was attacked by Kiowas.

How do, folks. Snuck up kinda quiet on me, didn't you? I guess you're the ones been asking around Fort Belknap about me—wanted to hear the legend of Britt Johnson and how I got my family back from the Comanches, right? Well, I leave the tellin' of that story to some of the other folks around here. I got all I can handle runnin' my business. I suppose I can tell you about how I saw an opportunity . . . and took it.

When I got my family back, I had to find a way to support 'em. The Civil War was over and lots of people were coming to the frontier to settle close to the forts, and everybody needed goods hauled. The way I saw it freighting would be the lifeblood of the frontier, so I started my own freight business between Weatherford and forts Richardson, Belknap and Griffin.

It was pretty tough in the first years. Plenty of folks were ready to make it hard for a black man

But, right now business is good. I got enough work that I need to get more wagons and I got some pretty good men out there driving for me. Even if it's just a big freighting wagon behind a team of mules, I'm helpin' change the frontier into the kind of place where folks can make a go of it in the world.

We haul plenty of stuff you'd expect . . . lumber, flour, just about anything folks need that they can't grow or make themselves. Corn's one of the main loads . . . for horse feed. Corn fed cavalry horses are faster than grass fed Indian ponies.

A man has to make a stand for the things he believes in. Me, I believe in the future of this part of Texas and I'm proud to be workin' to build it

Now you don't mind if I get back to work, do you? They're expecting me over at Jacksboro just three days from now. Take care.

Story of the Flat

The town of Fort Griffin, known as the Flat, was one of the wildest towns on the frontier.

The town grew up next to the fort on major trails crossing the Clear Fork of the Brazos River in the late 1860s. Here, soldiers, buffalo hunters, cowboys, Indians, settlers and outlaws rubbed shoulders for almost a decade.

Located just north of Albany, 43 miles northeast of present-day Abilene, the boomtown was a ramshackle collection of supply stores, stables, bordellos, and saloons.

For the most part, the town faded away in the late 1880s, as—one by one—the buffalo, longhorns and soldiers disappeared.

FAR LEFT: *Billy the Kid, outlaw and gunfighter*

UPPER LEFT: *John Wesley Hardin, outlaw and killer*

LOWER LEFT: *Bat Masterson, buffalo hunter and lawman*

FOLLOWING PAGE: *Mural Illustration for Frontier Texas by Andy Simmons*

1. *Fort Griffin*
2. *Conrad & Rath Store*
3. *Beehive Saloon*
4. *Indian Kate's*
5. *Echo News*
6. *Clampett Wagon Yard*
7. *Frankel's Store*
8. *Shiflett's Tannery*
9. *Louis Woolform's Bakery*
10. *Jail*
11. *Shannessy's Saloon*
12. *McGonigal House*
13. *Wilhem House*
14. *Pile of Buffalo Hides*
15. *Gleck Boot Shop*
16. *Charley Hatfield's Restaurant*
17. *Culp Brothers Hardware*
18. *Bowers Saloon*
19. *Pete Haverty's Livery*
20. *Planter's Hotel*
21. *Prostitute's cribs*
22. *Tonkawa Village*

"There was buffalo hunters, hide money, trail herd money and soldier money."

—John Chadbourne Irwin, remembering the Clear Fork frontier

"20 miles to Water
10 Miles to Wood
6 Inches to Hell
Make Yourself
at Home."

—written in charcoal on the door of an abandoned West Texas dugout

Frontier Legends at the Beehive Saloon

The Texas frontier attracted adventurous people, some escaping their past—or just escaping—and others who simply didn't fit well in civilized society.

There were good people, bad people, and some who could go either way. An outlaw in one town might be sheriff in the next.

The frontier was an untamed and lawless place—a magnet for wild and rambunctious characters. Many of these bigger-than-life characters have become American legends, featured in books, television series, and movies.

LEFT TO RIGHT:
Wyatt Earp, gambler and lawman

Doc Holliday, gambler and gunfighter

Butch Cassidy, bank robber

LEFT TO RIGHT:
Pat Garrett, buffalo hunter and lawman

Lottie Deno, gambler and poker player

Big Nose Kate, saloon owner

The Beehive Saloon Exhibit

"A killing was one of the ordinary, expected events of the night, on which comments were over and the incident closed by the time the blood had been mopped up from the floor."

—R. A. Slack, pioneer

Pat Garrett is portrayed by Michael Swanner, an actor with roles in The Newton Boys, Spy Kids II, Friday Night Lights *and other movies.*

Spirit Guide

Pat Garrett

Pat Garrett was born in 1850 in Alabama. At age 19, he began working on the LS Ranch in West Texas. Cattle rustling was rampant in the area, so Garrett's duties were that of a cowboy and a cattle gunman. In search of opportunity, he joined W. Skelton Glenn and worked as a buffalo hunter. However, the two had an argument over buffalo skins, and Garrett shot and killed Glenn in self-defense. Afterwards, Garrett moved to New Mexico, where he bought a saloon, and then was appointed Lincoln County Sheriff. It was during this career stint that Garrett hunted down and killed the infamous outlaw, Billy the Kid. Garrett was not re-appointed as sheriff, apparently because of the circumstances surrounding his shooting of the Kid, so he ranched for several years near Roswell, New Mexico, and later, he became a customs collector in El Paso, Texas.

Welcome to the Beehive Saloon. I'm just fillin' in here for Dutch. He's eatin' over at Skeeter's tent. My name is Pat Garrett and to get right to it, guess I'm best known for shootin' Billy the Kid. But, lots of things happened before me and Billy met in a pitch black room—when I had about two seconds to kill Billy before he killed me first, so that's what I did.

I come to Texas from Alabama after the Civil War. I done a bit of driftin', lots of us did. Those of us who made it to this old Texas frontier were a rough lot, I guess. We lived off Mother Nature and sometimes she was a stingy mama. She made you rough. I spent lots of nights here in the Beehive Saloon, just below Ft. Griffin. Doc Holliday and Wyatt Earp were here too, playing cards with the cowboys and buffalo hunters, and with soldiers from Griffin.

Back then, I was a buffalo hunter. You've probably seen those old Sharps buffalo guns like I used to shoot buffs for the skinners. Come down from Dodge City and I hunted all over this country. I could tell you some scary stories about how the Comanche chased us hunters back into Rath City or Griffin now and then—but, most folks want to hear about Billy the Kid. You'll likely hear plenty of versions of this story but I'm the man who lived it, so let me get on to it.

Well, it was like this. After the buffalo played out I drifted on out to Lincoln County, New Mexico. Had me a bar there, kinda like this Beehive. Billy was a customer... even a friend, sorta. He was a gun hand. Nice enough fellow, the senoritas shore liked him. Little guy, but he weren't no wet mop—he'd shoot you before you could say Jimmy Crack Corn. But, 'cept for stealin' now and then and 'coarse killing all those people, he didn't seem like a bad fellow. Some of those folks he shot probably even deserved it.

Anyway, folks in New Mexico got fed up with all the fighting and they hired me as sheriff—told me to bring in Billy, dead or alive. Well I trailed him a good while, down to Ft. Sumner. I rode up to the house of Pete Maxwell, Billy's friend, at night, thought I'd slip in and see if Billy was around. Of course, I had my pistol, and a shotgun, you know, the kind they carried on them Butterfield stagecoaches. It was pitch black inside that adobe house and I heard a bed creak as somebody got up—I eased the hammers back on that 10 gauge—made tiny clicks—course in that dark quiet room it sounded like you'd hit a skillet on an anvil—I could just feel a gun point at me from across the room in the blackness. When a voice whispered "Pete?" and I knew it was Billy and I shot him... I shot him in the dark. He never knew who killed him. Guess that was the end of the most famous outlaw in the west. Just doin' what I hired out to do.

Funny thing, I was a hero for a while after that, even wrote a book about 'ol Billy, but then I lost the next election for sheriff—guess people wanted to get shut of rough guys like me, wanted to be civilized.

(continued on next page)

It was . . . what's that word? A transition time. When civilization took hold, it really moved fast. Like Abilene town—it was started from nothing by the railroad. Same summer I killed Billy, and that was just 3 or 4 years after Col. McKenzie starved Quanah Parker and the Comanche onto reservations by shootin' up all their horses up in the Palo Duro.

Yep, the wild old days faded fast. And men like me and Wyatt and Doc and Bat Masterson, even the hardcase killers like Billy the Kid and John Wesley Hardin and them Indians like Satanta—just didn't fit with civilization. We were a holdover of wild times . . . bad times, I guess. This country was working on being peaceful, and it didn't want us around no more. And soon we warn't.

There's More to the Story

See pages 158–167 for information on these topics:

Butterfield Overland Mail

- Post by Coach
- Mail by Trail
- A Difficult Task
- Riding the Route

Towns and Social Life

- Forming Communities
- A Place to Call Home
- Making Neighbors
- For All That Ails You

Frontier Women

- Companions in Exile
- "Stand" by Their Man
- A Lonely Life
- A Life of Toil

Law and Lawlessness

- Outlaws and Gamblers
- Making the Frontier "Wild"
- A Blurry Boundary
- Cornerstone of Civilization

End of an Era

- An Industrial Nation
- The Machine on the Prairie
- Following the Rails

End of the Frontier

The railroad arrived in Abilene in 1881, bringing an end to the Texas frontier.

In March of that year, town sites were auctioned by the Texas & Pacific Railroad. Within two days, over 300 lots had been sold. Abilene was now officially established.

Soon churches and schools existed where the Indians, cowboys, buffalo hunters, soldiers and outlaws had recently roamed. City sidewalks covered the dangerous trails of the frontier.

The calm of civilization had arrived.

Well, not quite. Abilene's deputy sheriff was killed by a gunslinger in a saloon shootout in 1884.

LEFT: *Town Lot Sale Flyer*

FOLLOWING PAGE: *Photograph of steam locomotive, from the private collection of Willie Mae Pruitt Rogers. Donated by Nola Miles Rogers.*

"Abilene, Abilene,
Prettiest town I've ever seen;
Folks out there don't treat you mean
In Abilene, my Abilene."

—Bob Gibson and Les Brown, songwriters

One of the trains that first came into the new town of Abilene and pulled the curtain across the wild west in Texas.

Guns of the West

Guns changed the destiny of the wild frontier.

CHAPTER 7

The progression of firearms technology was a primary factor in winning the West.

The development of the "American Western Frontier" by settlers from the 1820s through the 1890s was achieved in great part through the ever-increasing power of personal firearms. These weapons gave their holder a distinct advantage over the fierce wildlife and native peoples they would encounter.

The Fort Phantom Hill Firearms Collection on display at Frontier Texas! shows the progression from early muzzle loading weaponry, all the way through the rapid-fire Winchesters and Colts.

The Evolution of Firearms

For centuries gunpowder weapons had been changing the course of battles around the globe. Each culture that gained the knowledge of gunpowder experimented with ways to improve its efficiency as a tool of hunting and war.

The demand for firearms from settlers moving westward across the plains helped lay the foundation for an American arms industry that would eventually fuel a bloody Civil War.

The competitive demands of the Civil War pushed the technological development of firearms. During the time of the Civil War, the Plains Indians stayed at the same technological level in weaponry. Going into the war, one soldier had about the same fire power as one Comanche warrior with a quiver of arrows. After the Civil War, one soldier was equal to about 12 Comanche warriors.

These photographs illustrate the constant quest by gun manufacturers to improve firearms, moving from the early flintlocks eventually to Winchester repeating rifles in heavy use on the frontier. But guns were expensive and in encounters involving Indians, outlaws or just disagreeing individuals, several stages of firearm development might be utilized.

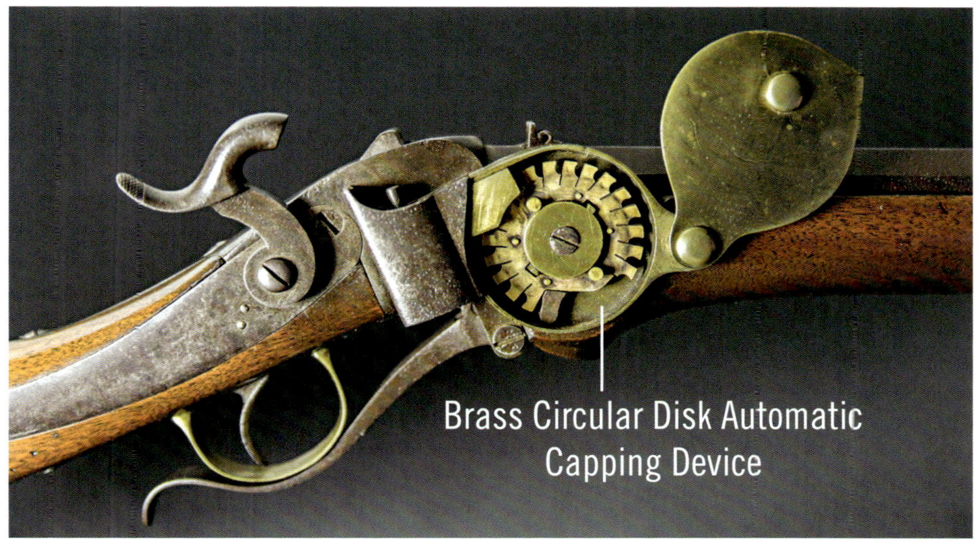

The Firearms Collection

The Fort Phantom Hill Foundation Firearms Collection was gathered over several decades from private collectors and public gun shows to show the significant types and varieties of firearms used on the Texas frontier. The foundation owns and maintains the Fort Phantom Hill historic site located north of Abilene, Texas.

"The technological advancements that happened during the Civil War in weaponry gave the soldiers a distinct advantage that was not going to be overcome by the Comanche Nation."

—Garland Richards, Fort Chadbourne (2013)

CHAPTER 8

Texas Icons

Four unique iconic sculptures greet visitors.

Testing the Texas Wind *by T. D. Kelsey*

The majesty of the great herds of buffalo, and then cattle, that once dominated the west Texas landscape is portrayed through magnificent works of art at Frontier Texas!

As you approach, you will be greeted by a massive sculpture of a buffalo bull, made of 109 separate cast bronze parts (including a heart!). It lets you appreciate the immensity of the animals that were the dominant mammal of the entire Great Plains area.

"Testing the Texas Wind"

Bronze Buffalo Sculpture by T. D. Kelsey (2003)

The heroic-sized (one and one half times life size) buffalo is the icon for Frontier Texas! It was chosen because the buffalo served as the primary economic resource for this region for thousands of years, losing that role just over a century ago. This sculpture is nine feet tall, and depicts a bull buffalo standing in the West Texas wind, surrounded by waving prairie grasses. It is hollow-cast bronze, meaning that there is a cavity in the center of the sculpture. It was sculpted in wax. Molds were then made and filled with melted bronze. After the cast surface was prepared, a special chemical solution was sprayed on the bronze to give it the present color and gloss, called a patina. The patina on the buffalo is "Cowboy Brown." The sculpture contains a bronze heart inside the buffalo, a trademark of this sculptor.

"Crossing Catclaw Creek"

Bronze Sculpture by T. D. Kelsey (2003)

The first sculpture created for Frontier Texas! had its origin many years before the facility would be built. This work was originally imagined to be built at a larger-than-life scale as the center of a public park. The dramatic 16-foot-long bronze by T. D. Kelsey depicts Anglo, Hispanic and Black cowboys driving eleven longhorn steers across Catclaw Creek, circa 1880. A recirculating fountain simulates the creek. The piece symbolizes the influence of the longhorns on this area and the importance of the Western, or Dodge City, Trail that crossed the site of Frontier Texas! More Texas longhorns were driven along the Western Trail than all other Texas cattle trails combined. The sculpture weighs 2800 pounds. Each animal possesses a bronze heart molded by the sculptor. The patina (the coloration) used on this bronze is called "Old World." Viewing these bronze cowboys, horses and longhorns as they fight their way across Catclaw Creek, one can almost hear the bellows, snorts and yells of the past as the trail drivers push the steers off the creek banks and across the running water.

"The Flying Buffalo Herd"

H. C. Zachry and Jack Rentz (2013)

Eight flat steel running buffalo mounted atop tall poles, rotating with the wind welcome visitors viewing the facility from the east. The concept was from H. C. Zachry and the structural design and fabrication was done by Jack Rentz and Rentech Boiler Systems, a local company that supports many civic activities. Each buffalo is 8' high and 12' long and weighs over 1000 pounds. As the breeze blows, each can rotate 360°. Seeing them move in the wind, almost 40' in the air, one can feel the drama of a mystical buffalo herd pounding through the sky. Spread over 250', the combined buffalo display creates the largest weathervane in the world!

"The Giant Buffalo Skull"

Steel and paint by Joe Barrington (2012)

Created by Texas artist Joe Barrington, this is one of the largest manufactured buffalo skulls in existence. At almost twenty feet between the horn tips, the huge steel skull can accommodate several kids at once to crawl through the eyes or climb on top for a photo.

Other Facility Exhibits

Longhorn Steer Head in Lobby

This is a real Texas longhorn raised by Fayette Yates of Abilene and donated to Frontier Texas! Fayette's grandfather, Cap Yates, is credited as one of the individuals who saved longhorns from complete extinction in the early part of the last century. This steer died at the age of 12. He was a big steer, weighing about 1600 pounds. His horn spread, tip to tip, is six and one half feet.

Unexpected Languages

Heard within the lobby restrooms, a narrator and three children—Anglo, Comanche and Hispanic—compare for visitors the English, Comanche and Spanish words for animals, family, greetings, counting and other subjects. Posey Liles of Lawton, Oklahoma, at age 10, provides the Comanche language segments of the audio. Posey's great-great-great-grandfather, Ten Bears, a Comanche chief, is featured pictorially in Frontier Texas!, as well as being quoted on one of the Seating Stones in the Parade Ground. This link was unknown at the time Posey was selected. Yuliana Prieto, at age 13, of Merkel is the talent for the Spanish words. Alex Warr, at age 11, of Abilene is the English voice. Betty Hukill of Abilene, Executive Director of the Paramount Theater is the voice of the announcer.

Story Stones

Twelve large blocks of limestone are engraved with quotes from people who lived on the frontier. The quotes on the six blocks in the front walkways of Frontier Texas! are more general, describing life on the frontier.

Six other stones are inside the courtyard, or parade ground, and they are more visceral in their description of people and events—reflecting more of the life and death struggle that often was a part of daily life in the prairies and canyons of West Texas.

A stroll through these stones is an experience that pulls the reader into the moments of happiness, fear, dread and melancholy of the people being quoted. Such a reading drives home the point that these were real, living, breathing people, often surviving in unimaginable circumstances.

Military Formation Stones

Concept developed by Don Frazier, PhD

These flat stones near the flagpole on the Parade Ground represent an infantry company at a Texas fort on Morning Parade. Constructed as an educational device for schoolchildren, the stones are arranged so that when a student stands on each, a typical company of a frontier fort is formed—officers in their proper position and everyone else in the location they would occupy in the standard military formation.

Additionally, each stone carries the name of each person's position—captains, sergeants and ranks. The stones also list the commanding officer of each of the frontier forts on the Texas Forts Trail and other information about the fort.

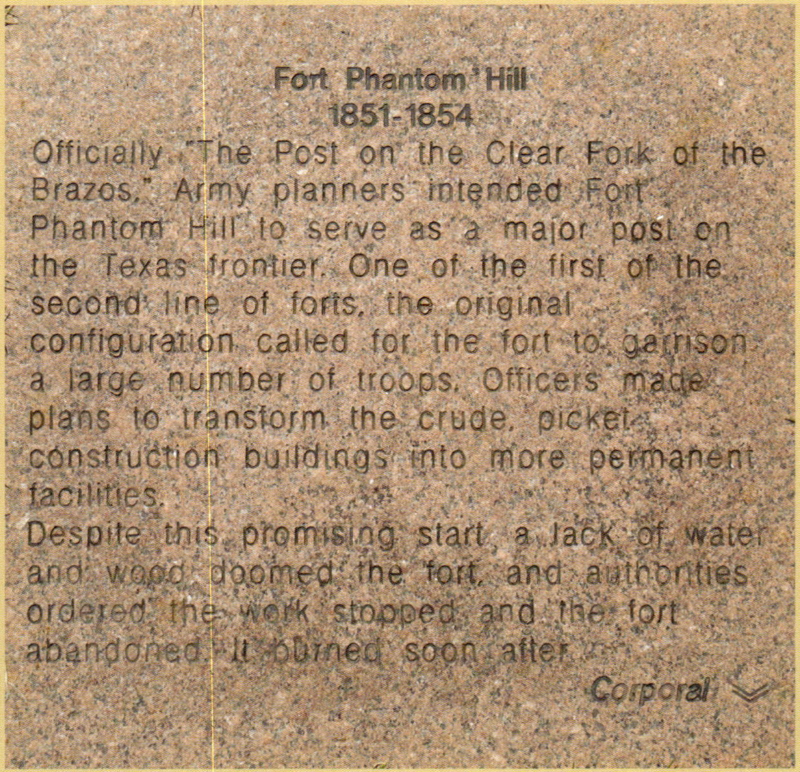

CHAPTER 9

There's More to the Story

Fourteen rotating information displays each covering four topics in more detail.

"To us, the buffalo was more than an animal. It was the stuff of life . . . no animal gave so much to the people."

—First Boy, Assiniboine

The Plains Indians consumed an average of three pounds of buffalo meat per person per day.

ROTATOR 1

Buffalo and Early Indians

Ancient Origins

Native American Ancestors

"A people enrich their minds who keep their history on the leaves of memory."

—Luther Standing Bear

People were present in North America long before European explorers "discovered" the "New World."

Indigenous tribes adapted well to changing environments and occupied a vast and rich country. Most experts agree that the first humans to set foot on American soil were Paleo-Indian hunters. These prehistoric peoples arrived during the last Ice Age by crossing a land bridge from Asia into North America. Ice-free corridors provided passage into the heart of the new continent where the immigrants and their descendants, the Native Americans, multiplied and spread.

The earliest Americans equipped themselves with tools made from stone, bone and wood and traveled extensively in search of big game and wild plant foods. Some were drawn to the Great Plains where the buffalo provided much of what they needed to survive as well as a spiritual focus for their lives.

Bountiful Buffalo

Hunting the Beast of Plenty

"To us, the buffalo was more than an animal. It was the stuff of life . . . no animal gave so much to the people."

—First Boy, Assiniboine

Huge herds of buffalo attracted prehistoric hunters to the Great Plains of America. In this land of rippling grasses and windblown clouds, native peoples found a source for many of the essentials of life—from food, fuel, clothing and shelter to tools, toys, containers and weapons. Traditionally, Indians hunted buffalo on foot.

They crept close, often in disguise, and aimed to kill without frightening the herd. At other times, they stampeded the beasts into narrow valleys or buffalo jumps where the panic-stricken animals became trapped or fell over cliffs. They also ambushed their prey with grass fires and at water holes. A hunt was an affair for the entire tribe. Men stalked and killed their quarry with spears or bows and arrows. Children waved blankets and made noises to force a stampede. Skinning and butchering the buffalo was work for the women.

Plains Indian culture coincided with the range of the buffalo. Nomadic tribes who depended on the beast for survival followed the great herds as they roamed the western landscape in search of grasses and water.

- A mature buffalo bull weighs approximately 2000 pounds while a grown buffalo cow weighs about 1100 pounds.
- Buffalo can run at speeds up to 35 miles per hour—three times faster than a human, but slower than a good horse.
- All buffalo have horns, which grow in yearly "rings" that can be used to tell an animal's age. On average, buffalo live 20–25 years.
- It is estimated that in prehistoric times, 60 million or more buffalo roamed the Great Plains.
- The Plains Indians consumed an average of three pounds of buffalo meat per person per day.
- Indians believed that killing buffalo for sport or pleasure was wasteful and an insult to the Great Spirit.

Cultural Remnants

People in Prehistoric Texas

"We have set up our lodges in these groves and swung our children from these boughs from time immemorial."

—Muguara, Penateka Comanche

People have lived in Texas since the end of the last Ice Age, more than 15,000 years. Cultural remnants, mainly projectile points and other stone tools, provide a glimpse of the early inhabitants who once roamed the plains in search of the great buffalo herds. Indians in prehistoric Texas developed special tools to hunt and trap animals, and for protection. The types of points they made are valuable "time markers" for culture change in different regions of the state.

Two major forms of projectile points have been found in Texas—dart points and arrow points. Dart points, the older of the two, were used to tip spears and weapons thrown with the atlatl or spear thrower. Arrow points, introduced with the bow and arrow some 700 years ago, were used to kill anything from birds to buffalo and humans. How these tools occur tells much about their ancient makers.

Early Indian Images

The Paint Rock Pictographs

"Pictograph illustrate how a vanished, nameless people perceived themselves and their world, their relation to God and to each other, and their fantasies and fears."

—W. W. Newcomb, Jr., Texas Indians authority

Some Texas Indians left a visual record of important events in their lives. At Paint Rock and other rock art sites around the state, primitive pictographs provide valuable insight into these native peoples. Paint Rock, 30 miles east of San Angelo, features over 1500 pictures painted on a cliff a half mile long and rising 70 feet above the Concho River.

Although their meaning is not always clear, the paintings hint at events such as tribal council meetings and war party raids. Depictions of birds, reptiles and animals, especially buffalo, suggest a dependence on area wildlife. Most impressive are dramatic indications that tribes such as the Jumano, Tonkawa, and later the Apache, Kiowa and Comanche, may have practiced astronomy.

- Pictographs are usually found on light-colored, protected surfaces. The limestone bluff at Paint Rock provided a perfect canvas for indigenous peoples to express themselves.
- The Indians used local minerals to produce their paint pigments. The predominant color at Paint Rock, red, was made from iron oxide.
- When Forrest Kirkland documented the Paint Rock pictographs over 70 years ago, he discovered that white is used only on two rocks.
- Through the centuries, images have been overlapped at Paint Rock. Experts believe that the designs painted in black are the oldest.

ROTATOR 2

Tribes of the Region

The Comanches

Lords of the Plains

"The Comanche excel all other nations in breeding, strength, valor, and gallantry."

—Athanase de Mézières, Spanish explorer, 1777

The Comanche Indians dominated the Texas frontier for almost 200 years. Their occupation was so complete that the land became known as Comanchería. Before 1700, the Comanches were essentially elements of the Shoshone tribe in the mountains of Wyoming. After acquiring horses brought to America by the Spaniards, the Comanches swept down upon the Southern Plains, driving out the Apaches and other tribes.

By the early 1800s, the Comanches were a powerful people with a population of about 20,000. Exceptional horsemen, they traveled in bands, following the buffalo herds and setting up tipi camps. Fiercely proud, they fought for their honor. Only after a long and bloody struggle were they forced onto the reservation. In 1875, weakened by warfare, disease and hunger, and fewer than 1600 in number, the Comanches succumbed to the will of the U.S. Government.

Major Comanche Bands

The Comanches ventured onto the Southern Plains not as a unified body but in numerous bands. The lack of a rigid tribal structure enabled the various groups to unite and separate, depending on the needs and goals of their members. In the 18th and 19th centuries, five

"Some of our chiefs make the claim that the land belongs to us. It is not what the Great Spirit told me. He told me that the land belongs to Him . . . and that I was not to forget to tell this to the white people."

—Kannekuk, Kickapoo prophet

The Kickapoos were unique in that they did not hunt buffalo. They did, however, have a reverence for hunting white-tail deer.

major bands emerged as the most important in Comanche history. Following Shoshone custom, the Comanche bands were often named for a type of food.

Kotsoteka Buffalo Eaters
Nokoni Wanderers
Penateka Honey Eaters
Quahadi Antelope Eaters
Yamparika Yap or Root Eaters

Legendary Comanche Leaders

Democratic principle was strongly implanted in Comanche political organization. Band members chose their leaders by common consent. A council of chiefs made all tribal decisions. Individuals, however, did not have to accept their opinions. They were free to leave and join another band. Consequently, Comanche bands were constantly changing in size and composition. Comanche leadership depended on the respect of the people, as well as an individual's popularity and influence. Peace chiefs were the oldest, wisest, kindest and most generous men. War chiefs were the most successful and admired warriors.

The Kiowas

Spiritual Warriors

"I love the land and the buffalo, and will not part with it . . . . I don't want to settle . . . when we settle down we grow pale and die."

—Satanta, "White Bear," Kiowa Chief

Originally from the Northern Great Plains and relatives of the Crow Indians, the Kiowas drifted south in the late 1700s. By the 1790s, they had joined into a lasting alliance with the Comanches. The Kiowas followed a simple tribal organization with a principal chief who dictated the course of his nation.

Deeply religious, the Kiowas conducted an annual Sun Dance to renew tribal unity. They also believed the power of a collection of sacred bundles, known as the ten grandmothers, kept them safe.

The 1866 death of the principal chief Dohäsan, or Little Mountain, unleashed a power struggle that pitted those who would accept a negotiated peace with the whites against those who were irreconcilable. Before long, the Kiowas rivaled their Comanche allies for spreading dread and mayhem on the Texas frontier. Their resistance, however, came to an end by 1875.

Koitsenko was a special society of warriors in the Kiowa tribe. To be a Koitsenko a Kiowa warrior had to show tremendous bravery and daring in battle. Every summer the Kiowas came together for the Sun Dance to restore the health of the tribe. They believed the sun was one of many spiritual forces.

Delawares, Kickapoos, and Tonkawas

Scouts and Nomads

"Some of our chiefs make the claim that the land belongs to us. It is not what the Great Spirit told me. He told me that the land belongs to Him . . . and that I was not to forget to tell this to the white people."

—Kannekuk, Kickapoo prophet

Known as the "Old Grandfather Tribe," the Delaware Indians originated along the Delaware River on the Atlantic coast. Elements of the tribe arrived in Texas in the early nineteenth century. Many Delawares served as scouts for the U.S. Army until most left for reservations in the Indian Territory in 1859.

The Kickapoo Indians originated in the Great Lakes region around Michigan. In 1864, they arrived in Texas on their way to settle in Mexico. Mistaken as the perpetrators of the Elm Creek Raid, they were attacked by state and Confederate forces at Dove

Creek. The Kickapoos won the battle and continued on to Mexico, but they were embittered toward the U. S. thereafter.

The Tonkawas originated as a Central Texas tribe that lived off the buffalo herds. Early on they sought peaceful relations with whites, and for years they served as scouts for the U.S. Army. In the 1850s, Delaware leader Jim Ned led Texas Rangers on attacks against Indians. Today, one of the creeks south of Abilene and an area school is named for Jim Ned. Jim Shaw, with three other Delawares, served as scouts and interpreters for U.S. Army forts Belknap and Phantom Hill in the 1850s. They received three times the pay of the typical private. The Kickapoos were unique in that they did not hunt buffalo. They did, however, have a reverence for hunting white-tail deer. Embittered by the unjust attack on them at Dove Creek in 1865, when the Kickapoos settled in Northern Mexico, they launched attacks against white settlers along the Rio Grande. In the early nineteenth century, Tonkawa warriors ceremonially cut off the hands and feet of slain enemies and ate them. This practice led enemies to particularly revile them. In 1862, warriors from the Delaware, Shawnee, and Caddo tribes slaughtered 135 out of the remaining 309 Tonkawas. Reportedly, the massacre was revenge for Tonkawas having eaten a couple of Shawnees.

Warfare and Ceremony

A Culture of Honor

"No people probably on the face of the earth . . . entertain a higher appreciation for the deeds of the daring and successful warrior, than the North American savages."

—Captain Randolph B. Marcy, U. S. Army

Leadership among the Comanches and Kiowas depended upon prestige and respect gained by warfare. Both societies valued courage and prowess in warriors and expected their leaders to be adept at leading war parties. Any Comanche warrior could lead a war party, but his prestige and success in past combat determined who would follow him. Similarly, Kiowa war parties were led by respected leaders. Both tribes tended to strike quickly and withdraw swiftly. If pursued, they could split up into smaller groups and escape.

Both the Comanches and Kiowas held great respect for acts of courage in battle. "Counting coup," a practice among many of the Plains Indians, celebrated individual acts of bravery. The most revered coup was given to the warrior who could touch or strike a living enemy. Through such acts, warriors could rise quickly in power within the tribe.

"I was born upon the prairie, where the wind blew free . . . . I want to die there and not within walls . . ." —Paruasuumarunu., "Ten Bears," Comanche Chief

"Strategy loses its advantages against an enemy who accepts few or none of the conventionalities of civilized warfare." —Edward S. Farrow, 21st U.S. Infantry

"They seemed to like Mexican captives, because they could raise them up and no one could tell them from full blood Indians." —Jeff Smith, Comanche captive

"A long time ago this land belonged to our fathers; but when I go up to the river I see camps of soldiers on its banks. These soldiers . . . kill my buffalo and when I see that, my heart feels like bursting." —Satanta, Kiowa chief

". . . he who can count the greatest number of scalps is the most highly honored by his tribe. This idea is inculcated from their earliest infancy." —Captain Randolph B. Marcy, U. S. Army

"A long time ago this land belonged to our fathers; but when I go up to the river I see camps of soldiers on its banks. These soldiers . . . kill my buffalo and when I see that, my heart feels like bursting."

—Satanta, Kiowa chief

Deeply religious, the Kiowas conducted an annual Sun Dance to renew tribal unity. They also believed the power of a collection of sacred bundles, known as the ten grandmothers, kept them safe.

> *A capable man could skin fifty buffalo a day, and usually was paid $50 a month. I have paid as much as twenty-cents a hide to a good skinner."*
>
> —Billy Dixon, buffalo hunter

> *By 1879 the buffalo were almost extinct. Many hunters, like the Mooars, earned enough money to remain in Texas after the slaughter to begin cattle businesses.*

ROTATOR 4

Commercial Buffalo Hunting

Where the Buffalo Roam

Commercial Hunting Begins

"There was much science to killing a buffalo."

—J. Wright Mooar, buffalo hunter

In 1870, innovations in hide tanning techniques meant that tens of millions of buffalo became vulnerable to hunters seeking their fortunes. Brothers J. Wright and John W. Mooar typified the more than 1500 hunting teams that poured onto the Kansas plains as a result. In 1872, the Mooar brothers and others desired to follow the herds into the Texas Panhandle, an area reserved for Plains Indians hunting according to the Medicine Lodge Treaty of 1867. They asked permission from Col. R. I. Dodge, commander of Fort Dodge, who told them to "hunt buffalo where the buffalo are." In 1874, the Mooars and hundreds of others moved farther into the Texas frontier to begin killing the southern bison herd. By 1879 the buffalo were almost extinct. Many hunters, like the Mooars, earned enough money to remain in Texas after the slaughter to begin cattle businesses.

Buffalo Math

- Number of American bison in North America before the Plains Indians acquired horses—between 30 million and 60 million.
- Number of American bison killed in Kansas and Texas between 1868 and 1881—between 20 million and 31 million.
- Number of American bison in the United States in 1889—541.
- Number of American bison in North America today—150,000 to 200,000.

The Hunt Begins

The Shooters

"The man I sold my old .44 to killed 119 buffalo in one day with it. That beats me with my Big .50—as 93 is the most that I ever killed in one day."

—R. W. Snyder, buffalo hunter

A typical hunting team consisted of around four men and included at least one shooter accompanied by skinners and perhaps a camp manager and teamster. During a typical day, the group would scout for a herd, pick out a small clump of animals, and approach them downwind as close as possible. The shooter would then set up a "stand" or firing position, and, using something to brace his gun, begin the work. The shooter would try to identify the lead bull, then "shoot his ball in his side so that it would not go through," wrote hunter W. Skelton Glenn. By mortally wounding the animal but not killing it outright, the hunter avoided spooking the herd. As this animal stumbled about, the other animals would not be concerned, allowing them to be taken systematically while they rested. In this manner, each team killed between fifty and a hundred buffalo per day.

Buffalo hunters preferred large-bore rifles that loaded quickly and fired accurately. The most-used buffalo rifles were:

- *Trapdoor Springfield*—nicknamed the "needle gun" because of its long, slender firing pin, the Trapdoor Springfield fired .50–70 cartridges and was quite successful in killing bison.

- *Remington Rolling Block*—this rifle fired .50–70 and .45–70 cartridges, and was preferred by many hunters because of its relative ease in loading.
- *Sharps "Big Fifty"*—The Sharps Model 1874 (actually introduced in 1871) was the rifle most famous and most used in the buffalo slaughter. Firing .50–70 and .50–90 cartridges, this weapon was billed as a rifle that "fires today and hits tomorrow." Although only 6001 were ever manufactured, the "Big Fifty" was the quintessential buffalo rifle.

Ready to Harvest

The Skinners

"I came to learn that skinning was a dirty, disagreeable, laborious, uninspiring job."

—Frank H. Mayer, buffalo hunter and skinner

An integral part of the buffalo hunting team was the skinner. The purpose of the hunt was to "harvest" the hides. "The best skinner . . . prided himself on being able to skin from fifty to sixty buffalo a day, without regarding it as an extra heavy day's job," wrote hunter's wife Sophie Poe. After the last carcass of a group of buffalo hit the ground, the skinners went to work. The skinners would began taking the hides, using their wagon and mules to peel the animals and roll the heavy bodies over. These men did heavy work and were covered in the gore associated with processing large game. The speed in which they worked dictated how many animals could be taken in a day. As the season progressed, the plains of West Texas became dotted with the rotting carcasses of buffalo, stripped of their hides but their meat and bones left for scavengers.

Firsthand Accounts

"I always did my own killing and generally had two experienced men to do the skinning. A capable man could skin fifty buffalo a day, and usually was paid $50 a month. I have paid as much as twenty-cents a hide to a good skinner." —Billy Dixon, buffalo hunter

"We fastened a forked stick to the center of the hind axle-tree of a wagon, letting the end drag on the ground on an incline of say 20 degrees; fastened a chain or rope to the same axle, then we would . . . hook the loose end of the chain over a front leg. After skinning the upper side down, then start the team up and pull the dead animal up a little and stop. (The stick prevented the wagon from backing up.) Then we would skin the belly down midsides; start the team again, and pull the carcass over; having rolled the first side of the hide close to the backbone. Then we would skin down to the backbone, and the hide was separated from the carcass. We would then throw the hide in the wagon, and proceed as before until all the hides were skinned from the dead carcasses." —John R. Cook, buffalo hunter and skinner

Many Ways to Profit

The Suppliers

"There was buffalo hunters, hide money, trail herd money and soldier money."

—John Chadbourne Irwin, resident of Fort Griffin

With the influx of hunters, the Texas frontier presented tremendous opportunity for entrepreneurs who recognized the potential. By 1874, Fort Griffin had become the base of operations for hundreds of buffalo hunters. Frank Conrad, a merchant in the town and sutler to the fort, became one of the greatest beneficiaries as stores like his fueled the hunting industry.

The men who started it all, J. Wright and John W. Mooar, along with a freighter named Pete Snyder, moved their base to Fort Griffin as well. Soon, Kansas hide firms opened branch offices. Charles Rath followed suit, establishing Rath City sixty miles west of Fort Griffin. Other sites also featured merchants and hide buyers, such as Buffalo Gap, Fort Phantom Hill, and Mobeetie. Buyers flocked to these places to purchase the hides, then consign them to freighters to get them to shipping points. In the fall of 1876, a man entered Frank Conrad's store at Fort Griffin and asked for three kegs of gunpowder and four hundred pounds of lead.

Below is Conrad's recollection of the event:

"It nearly took my breath away. I asked him if he was shooting artillery and what his occupation was. He said he was a buffalo hunter. I told him that I had only two-thirds a keg, and as a general thing only sold a keg in three months. I . . . found he was the forerunner of a lot of Kansas men coming to Texas to kill buffalo . . . I decided to send to Bridgeport, Connecticut, after twenty-five kegs, and before it came, there were men who arrived that would have taken twice as much."

The speed in which [the skinners] worked dictated how many animals could be taken in a day. As the season progressed, the plains of West Texas became dotted with the rotting carcasses of buffalo, stripped of their hides but their meat and bones left for scavengers.

"Twelve Indian heads, minus hair, feathers and other thump min, now adorn the gateposts of the corral."

—J. T. Marshall, witnessing aftermath of Battle of Adobe Walls

Scalping was not always fatal, and some victims survived. Once taken, the scalp became a revered sacrifice, subject of triumphal dance, or was used as a pendant or amulet.

ROTATOR 5

Conflict

Government Policy

Peacekeeping and Pacifying

"Send them powder and lead, if you will, and for the sake of lasting peace, let them kill, skin, and sell until they have exterminated the buffalo."

—General Philip Sheridan, 1875

With the establishment of a peacetime military force in 1815, the U.S. Army played the role of peacekeeper between Indian and settler. Beginning in 1830, the Indians were simply moved westward past the line of forts that marked the Permanent Indian Frontier. After the Mexican War, the spirit of manifest destiny propelled settlers into lands still occupied by Indians, and Texas was no exception. Between 1848 and 1860, the army engaged in more than 84 skirmishes in efforts to maintain peace by confining Indians to reservations.

Attitudes changed following the Civil War. After experience with total war, Army officers had lost any sense of sympathy and began applying lessons learned in defeating the Confederacy to suppressing the Indian. By 1880, the strategy of exhaustion was successful, and the Indian ceased to be a threat to frontier Texans. Prior to 1848, there were only three significant engagements between the U.S. Army and the western tribes. After the decades after the Mexican War, the number jumped to more than three hundred. Prior to the Civil War, the year in which the greatest number of skirmishes was fought was 1857, in which there were 19 clashes. This was followed by 1850, with 18. Between 1866 and 1880, the U.S. Army fought with Indians on 134 separate occasions. Most of these engagements (117) were fought by mounted soldiers.

Quanah Parker

Antagonist or Accommodationalist

"My band is not going to live on the reservation. Tell the white chiefs that the Quahadi are warriors."

—Quanah Parker, 1867

Quanah Parker was born around 1845 in the Wichita Mountains of what is now Oklahoma. The son of Comanche leader Peta Nocona and white captive Cynthia Ann Parker, he would grow to become a man of two worlds. When his father was killed in 1860, Parker became a leader among the Quahadi Comanches, and the tribe emerged to dominate much of the Texas plains. Beginning in 1871, the U.S. Army began tracking Parker and his followers. Following the Battle of Adobe Walls, Parker realized the futility of continued resistance, and moved to Indian Territory.

Becoming one of the wealthiest Indians in America, Parker refused to totally adopt white ways, and encouraged other Indians to maintain their cultural heritage. He did, however, work with white ranchers to allow them to lease Comanche land for pasturing, and became a well-known advocate for cooperation. When Quanah Parker finally settled on the reservation, he did his best to live in peace with the neighboring white settlers. In addition to operating his ranch, he continued to be a spokesman for his people. In 1902 his people made him Deputy Sheriff of Lawton, Oklahoma. Quanah Parker was active in the peyote-eating Native American Church, and encouraged the use of peyote by Indians in Oklahoma. Parker had five stars painted on the roof of his ranch home, to ensure that he had more stars than any army general

"Resting here until day breaks and shadows fall and darkness disappears." —Inscription on Quanah Parker's original gravestone.

Controlling the Tribes

Choices Facing a Chief

"The Government of the United States desires peace, and its honor is here pledged to keep it. The Indians desire peace, and they now pledge their honor to maintain it."

—Medicine Lodge Treaty with the Kiowas and Comanches, October 1867

From Texas independence forward, Comanches and other Indians in Texas struggled for survival. As settlers made their way west, tribal leaders were challenged in their efforts to maintain their traditional nomadic lifestyle. The result was conflict as both sides fought for dominance of the Texas frontier.

Chiefs had three options. Accommodation could alienate the remainder of the tribe. Resistance might bring about the death of the tribe. A blending of the two extremes might yield more favorable results and the preservation of tribal autonomy. All were tried with varying levels of success. Regardless, by 1880, the chiefs found their authority limited. No longer were their people free to travel the great distances they had known in the past. They were confined to reservations and forced to live the white man's ways.

The Comanches were known for their fierceness, and clashed with Texans, the U. S. Army, and even Buffalo Hunters. Although most clashes with the Comanches are best called minor skirmishes involving a handful of Indians and white settlers or soldiers, a few engagements warrant being called battles:

- Battle of Plum Creek, August 1840—Comanches versus Texas Rangers near present-day Lockhart.
- Elm Creek Raid, October 1864—Kiowas and Comanches raid into settlements in Parker County. Fought settlers and elements of the Confederate Border Regiment.
- Adobe Walls, June 1874—Comanches and Kiowas under Quanah Parker and Isa-Tai versus a group of buffalo hunters.
- Red River Campaign, June 1874–Spring 1875—Comanches, Kiowas, Southern Cheyennes and Arapahos versus the U. S. Army along the Llano Estacado.

Tough Attitudes

Life and Death Struggles

"There were several scalps . . . [taken] as a lesson to the Indians. It seemed that by using their own tactics against them, they were more terrified; at least that is what was claimed by the white men."

—Sallie Reynolds Matthews, Texas pioneer

Although there are those who claim that early European colonists taught Indians to scalp, archaeological evidence suggests that scalping was common well before contact. Europeans had originally cut off people's heads for trophies, but found scalps easier to preserve and transport, and they eventually embraced the Indian practice. By the French and Indian War (1754–1763), the English offered bounties for the scalps of enemies. Between 1835 and 1880, Mexican authorities encouraged the practice, paying private armies to kill Indians, with scalps serving as receipts. Scalps were usually taken from the dead, although some Plains Indians preferred a live victim. Scalping was not always fatal, and some victims survived. Once taken, the scalp became a revered sacrifice, subject of triumphal dance, or was used as a pendant or amulet.

Life on the frontier was one of violence. Fighting between whites and Indians was without mercy. By the end of the conflict, Texans conducted themselves in a manner not unlike that of the Indians they fought against:

"Twelve Indian heads, minus hair, feathers and other thump min, now adorn the gateposts of the corral."—J. T. Marshall, witnessing aftermath of Battle of Adobe Walls

"When we fell into [Indian] hands they scalped us and frightfully mutilated our bodies, frequently cutting and hacking us to pieces. We didn't do as bad as that but scalped them just the same. Indian scalps in ranger camps were as common as pony tracks." —Major John B. Jones, Texas Rangers' Frontier Battalion

"Resting here until day breaks and shadows fall and darkness disappears."

—Inscription on Quanah Parker's original gravestone.

ROTATOR 6

Troopers of the Plains

Doughboys and Pony Soldiers

The Frontier Army in Texas

"The giant arms of the United States would soon sweep the few bands of hostile Indians from our borders"

—*Houston Democratic Telegrapher and Texas Register*, 10 December 1845

In the aftermath of the Mexican War, the United States assumed peacekeeping duties in Texas. Some in the state advocated federal support for the Texas Rangers, but the task of maintaining good relations fell to the Army. Between 1848 and 1860, as many as 4000 U. S. regulars were ordered to Texas. By the end of the Civil War, 39,000 were in place, but this soon dwindled to pre-war numbers as reconstruction came to an end. From 1867 to 1880, the state returned to the pre-war standard of approximately 4000 troops in any given year.

With the concentration of the Kiowas and Comanches to the reservation, the need for soldiers on the Texas frontier steadily declined. In fulfilling their duties, the army played a major role in the development of the Texas frontier and its economy, flooding the cash-poor state with hard currency.

Low pay and inadequate rations plagued the U. S. army. Some examples of these problems:

- In 1870, Congress instituted an across-the-board pay cut for all enlisted grades, which reduced a private's pay from $16 to $13 per month. The next year, 8800 troops, 32.6 percent of the Army's enlisted personnel, deserted.
- Daily rations for an enlisted man consisted of: $^{3}/_{4}$ lb. pork or bacon OR 1 $^{1}/_{4}$ lb. of fresh or salt beef; 18 oz. bread or flour OR 12 oz. hard bread OR 1 $^{1}/_{4}$ lb. corn meal.
- For every hundred rations, soldiers also received: 4 lbs. soap, 1 $^{1}/_{2}$ lbs. candles, 2 qts. salt, 4 qts. vinegar, 8 qts. peas or beans, 6 lbs. coffee, and 12 lbs. sugar.
- In an 1853 effort to combat scurvy, it was suggested that troops at Fort Phantom Hill and other frontier posts supplement their otherwise monotonous rations with pickles.

A Brittle Sword

Manpower

"We enlist men . . . without knowing their names, residences, or anything whatever about them. Is it strange that a third of our Army deserts each year?"

—Colonel William B. Hazen, Sixth Infantry, 1872

Since the establishment of the United States, the American people always viewed a standing army in peacetime with disdain. Throughout the nineteenth century, few native-born Americans would willingly enlist, preferring the more republican militia or volunteers.

The 1877 *New York Sun* described America's defenders as "bummers, loafers, and foreign paupers." While many enlistees were from the dregs of society, immigrants frequently saw the U. S. Army as a place of opportunity, using the military to learn English, move west, and make a name for themselves.

The nineteenth century army was also culturally diverse. In addition to Irish and German enlisted men, it was common to see Indian scouts and black teamsters and servants employed at a frontier post. Regardless of its rough appearance, the army ultimately accomplished the gargantuan task placed before it.

In the aftermath of the Mexican War, the army continued to draw upon its traditional sources—the destitute, the disoriented, and the naïve:

The army played a major role in the development of the Texas frontier and its economy.

"The giant arms of the United States would soon sweep the few bands of hostile Indians from our borders."

—*Houston Democratic Telegrapher and Texas Register*, 10 December 1845

- During the 1850s, twice as many immigrants enlisted as did native-born Americans. Most immigrants were recent arrivals who had not yet adjusted to American life Approximately 50% were from Ireland, and 20% from Germany.
- Delaware and Tonkawa scouts were employed by the U. S. Army on the Texas Frontier. During the 1874–75 Red River War, more than a dozen Tonkawas, under the command of Lieutenant Peter Boehm, aided Ranald S. Mackenzie in his efforts to confine the Kiowas and Comanches.

Dawn to Dusk

A Soldier's Life

"The troops at Fort Phantom Hill present a very busy, industrious appearance, digging, chopping, sawing, hauling, and pulling."

—Lt. Clinton Lear, Fifth Infantry, 1851

The soldier's life was anything but easy. Reveille came before sunrise, and taps concluded a day that was consumed with drill, guard mount, patrol, and construction duties as soldiers were initially responsible for building the posts they were to occupy. A soldier's life was monotonous, best described by long periods of boredom punctuated by brief moments of sheer terror. Death was always a possibility, though rarely from Indians, as illness and disease were much more prevalent, a consequence of poor diet and difficult living conditions.

Military posts often formed the nucleus of frontier settlements, attracting a wide variety of personalities who lived within view of the garrison. These communities frequently outlived the posts they relied upon for protection, and many early Texas towns listed numerous former soldiers among their inhabitants. A military day was dictated by the "sounding of bugle calls" that frequently began before sun-up. Ten days after the arrival of the first troops at Fort McKavett in 1869, the schedule was as follows:

Reveille – 5:30 A.M.
Stable Call – Immediately thereafter
Breakfast Call – 6:15 A.M.
Surgeon's Call – 6:30 A.M.
Fatigue Call – 7:00 A.M.
Guard Mount – 8:00 A.M.
Recall from Fatigue – 12:00 Noon
Dinner Call – 12:15 P.M.
Orderly Call – 1:00 P.M.
Fatigue Call – 1:00 P.M.
Stable Call – 5:30 P.M.
Retreat – Sunset
Tattoo – 8:30 P.M.
Taps – 9:00 P.M.

Life at the Top

Those in Command

"The most promising young officer in the army."

—General U. S. Grant, on Brigadier General of Volunteers Ranald S. Mackenzie, 1864

In the nineteenth century, U. S. Army officers came from three sources: West Point, civilian society, or from the ranks. The vast majority of officers serving prior to 1860 were graduates of West Point.

Civilians had been commissioned as early as 1832, but it was not until the Civil War that they became officers in significant numbers. The influx of this huge block of officers, all roughly the same age, created a bulge in the officer corps.

Those who received commissions after the Civil War soon found their path to promotion blocked by those commissioned prior to 1867. With no mandatory retirements or promotions within regiments, some men remained lieutenants for twenty years or more. The result was a constant scramble among officers to find special duties or activities to distinguish themselves and win them one of the few merit-based promotions.

Army command throughout the 19th century was somewhat disjointed, in that there were two parallel lines of command, one for the line (combat troops) and another for the staff (support elements).

- The General in Chief commanded the line regiments, but was dependent upon the Secretary of War, who oversaw the staff departments (adjutant general, judge advocate general, commissary general, paymaster general, chief of ordnance, provost marshal, inspector general, quartermaster general, surgeon general, chief of engineers, and chief signal officer).
- 42% of the 3598 commissions granted between 1865 and 1898 were given out between 1865 and 1867. Of these, 88% went to ex-Civil War volunteers.

A soldier's life was monotonous, best described by long periods of boredom punctuated by brief moments of sheer terror.

"Such a country as this I almost wish I had never seen it . . . . I don't believe it was ever intended for civilized people, it was made for wild Indians and buffalo."

—Susan Emily Bartholomew, settler at Fort Davis in Shackelford County

Conflicts arose between the neighboring settlers and the reservation Indians, with both sides guilty of plundering, raiding and taking captives.

ROTATOR 7

Frontier Forts

Securing the Frontier

First Line of Forts

"The white man and the red man cannot dwell in harmony together. Nature forbids it . . . ."

—Mirabeau B. Lamar, 1839, President of the Republic of Texas

Defending the Texas Frontier was not an easy task. Inhabiting the region were some of the greatest guerrilla fighters of all time—the Comanche, Kiowa, Apache and Lipan tribes—who resented intruders. When the Spanish attempted to colonize the area in the 1700s, and establish missions to "save the aborigine's soul," troops had to be sent to protect Spain's interests. Indian hostilities continued to rise even after Spain withdrew and the frontier came under Mexican rule in 1821.

When Texas declared its independence from Mexico in 1836, the new republic struggled to safeguard its borders. A small regiment of ten companies totaling 560 men proved grossly inadequate. After the annexation of Texas in 1845, the federal government established a line of military forts to secure the state's boundaries, restrain the Indians and protect the frontier settlements.

Charged with keeping the peace and promoting western expansion, frontier forts also served an important economic role. Towns sprang up in their shadows, and the army became the chief consumer of goods from area merchants, farmers and ranchers.

First Line of Federal Forts (1848–1849)

The first forts in Texas constructed by the U. S. Army stretched between the Red River and the Rio Grande, following the 1848–1849 line of frontier settlement. Forts Brown and Polk were an exception, having been established before the Mexican War. Many Texas forts were built to protect settlers and travelers against Indian forays. Fort Bliss, at El Paso, was also required to protect the international border between Texas and Mexico from marauding tribes.

Fort Bliss, 1848–present
Fort Martin Scott, 1848–1853
Fort Ringgold, 1848–1944
Fort Croghan, 1849–1855
Fort Duncan, 1849–1883
Fort Gates, 1849–1852
Fort Graham, 1849–1853
Fort Inge, 1849–1869
Fort Lincoln, 1849–1852
Fort McIntosh, 1849–1946
Fort Worth, 1849–1853

Additional Fortifications

Second and Third Lines

"Such a country as this I almost wish I had never seen it . . . . I don't believe it was ever intended for civilized people, it was made for wild Indians and buffalo."

—Susan Emily Bartholomew, settler at Fort Davis in Shackelford County

The lure of low cost land, economic opportunity and gold enticed pioneers and adventurers to head west in the mid-1800s. It didn't take long for the wave of immigration to roll past the first line of Texas forts. As settlers advanced farther west and onto Indian hunting grounds, troubles erupted. By the 1850s, the U. S. Government found it necessary to establish a second line of forts to guard the expanding frontier. A new policy was also needed to address the escalating Indian problem. A plan to curtail Indian movements by pushing them onto reservations near Fort Belknap in West Texas proved unsuccessful. Conflicts arose between the neighboring settlers and the reservation Indians, with both sides guilty of plundering, raiding and taking captives. As tensions mounted, uneasiness permeated the plains. A third line of forts did little to assuage the fears of settlers on the frontier. Civilian settlement soon moved beyond the established line of posts, necessitating the creation of new forts farther west.

Second Line of Federal Forts (1850–1854)

Plans for a second line of fortifications seemed adequate in theory, but in reality all of the frontier posts were too far apart and their garrisons too small to completely patrol the Lone Star State. The average strength of most forts was fewer than 90 men. As the line of settlement moved westward, it became necessary to close some forts and build new ones on the advancing frontier.

Fort Merrill, 1850–1855
Fort Belknap, 1851–1867
Fort Mason, 1851–1869
Fort Phantom Hill, 1851–1870
Fort Chadbourne, 1852–1872
Fort Clark, 1852–1946
Fort Ewell, 1852–1854
Fort McKavett, 1852–1883
Fort Terrett, 1852–1854
Fort Davis, 1854–1891

Third Line of Federal Forts (1855–1860)

Fort Lancaster, 1855–1874
Camp Cooper, 1856–1861
Fort Quitman, 1858–1882
Fort Stockton, 1859–1886

The Post War Years

Return to Law and Order

"Texas has not yet suffered from the war and will require some intimidation."

—Major General Philip H. Sheridan, 1865,
Military commander of Texas and Louisiana

Following the Civil War, the United States was more interested in re-establishing its authority over Texas than in protecting the frontier. During the nine years of Reconstruction, the state was in turmoil. Marshall law was imposed and frontiersmen were not allowed to raise arms or organize for their defense.

As news of continuing Indian raids reached Washington, U. S. troops once again occupied posts along the frontier. Some forts were beyond repair or in undesirable locations. A number of new posts were established farther west and north.

Troops garrisoned at these forts fought Indians, defended the Texas border from foreign invasion and smuggling, maintained law and order, conducted scientific research and performed civil engineering duties. The forts themselves provided jobs, commerce, culture and education to the surrounding civilian population. In 1861, after Texas seceded from the Union and Civil War erupted, federal troops withdrew from the frontier. Settlers, left without protection, banded together in civilian picket forts. In 1864, news of a murderous Indian attack at Elm Creek caused fear to become rampant. Many pioneer families abandoned their homesteads and fled eastward. Federal forces did not return to the frontier until after the war.

Post War Forts in Texas (1867–1881)

Fort Richardson, 1867–1878
Fort Concho, 1867–1889
Fort Elliott, 1875–1890
Fort Griffin, 1867–1881
Camp Pena Colorado, 1879–1893
Fort Hancock, 1881–1895

Peace and Prosperity

Taming the Frontier

"... it would be wise to invite all the sportsmen of England and America ... for a Grand Buffalo Hunt, and make one grand sweep of them all."

—Generals William Tecumseh Sherman and
Philip Sheridan regarding Indian Policy, 1869

The coming of the buffalo hunters in the 1870s marked an era of prosperity in West Texas. Hunters swarmed onto the plains, fueling the growth of towns like Fort Griffin, which served as a major supply, hide processing and transportation center. Despite warnings to Washington concerning the wholesale slaughter of the buffalo, no steps were taken to curb the hunters' zeal. Soon, the great herds were gone and the Indians were left without their major food source. In the face of starvation, many Indians moved onto the reservation. Some, however, did not go quietly.

In 1874, in an act of defiance, Comanche, Cheyenne and Kiowa warriors attacked a hunter's camp near Adobe Walls in the Texas Panhandle. The army's response was a ten-month campaign known as the "Red River War," which finally neutralized the Indian threat on the frontier. With peace established, frontier forts no longer had a real purpose. In the 1880s, most were abandoned.

"The [black] troops seemed especially proud of their uniform and of their profession as soldiers."

—Post Surgeon, Fort Davis, 1877

The Buffalo Soldiers made significant and lasting contributions to the settlement of the desolate and dangerous Texas frontier.

ROTATOR 8

Buffalo Soldiers

Fighting for Freedom

Origins

"Let the black man get upon his person the brass letters U. S. . . . [and] there is no power on Earth which can deny that he has earned the right to Citizenship."

—Frederick Douglass, antislavery activist

African Americans had fought in American wars since the War for American Independence. However, the creation of the "Buffalo Soldier" regiments marked their first formal entry into the U. S. Army in peacetime. On 28 July 1866, Congress created six regular regiments for black enlisted men: the 9th and 10th Cavalry, and the 38th, 39th, 40th, and 41st Infantry Regiments. Early enlistees in the black regiments came from the former slave states, and saw the military as a place of opportunity. They took pride in their service, and served with distinction.

Despite their desire to serve their country, the buffalo soldiers were frequently subjects of racial prejudice, supplied with outdated and cast-off equipment, and faced considerable hostility from white officers and civilians throughout their tenure on the frontier. In May 1863, the War Department established the Bureau of Colored Troops to oversee the formation of black regiments for the Union Army. Although recognized by the U. S. government, these black soldiers often faced prejudice from white officers and soldiers alike. By the end of the war, more than 140 regiments of United States Colored Troops (U.S.C.T.) had been raised, and included infantry, cavalry, and heavy and light artillery.

Before the Civil War was over, some 180,000 African Americans had fought in all major theaters of operation and suffered almost 38,000 casualties. Most historians agree that the U.S.C.T. played an integral role in the ultimate Union victory.

Black Men in Army Blue

The Regiments

"The [black] troops seemed especially proud of their uniform and of their profession as soldiers."

—Post Surgeon, Fort Davis, 1877

As the Army renewed its efforts to maintain peace in the post-Civil War United States, it was reorganized to allow it to more effectively perform its task. In 1869, the authorized strength of the Army was reduced from 54,641 to 37,313 men. As a result of these changes, the all-black Thirty-eighth and Forty-first Infantry Regiments were merged into the Twenty-fourth Infantry Regiment, and the Thirty-ninth and Fortieth became the Twenty-fifth Infantry. Along with the Ninth and Tenth Cavalry, these units carried the "Buffalo Soldier" nickname.

The Buffalo Soldiers made significant and lasting contributions to the settlement of the desolate and dangerous Texas frontier. They protected settlers from Indian attacks, built roads and erected telegraph lines; and performed escort duty for the postal carriers, stage lines, and survey parties.

Why "Buffalo Soldier"?

The nickname "Buffalo Soldiers" was initially bestowed upon troopers of the Tenth Cavalry, the term was ultimately applied to all black troops on the frontier. The most common explanation given for the origin of this name is that the Indians saw a similarity between the hair of the African American soldier and the buffalo. The sacred nature of the buffalo to the Plains Indians meant that they would only bestow the name on worthy adversaries. The proud acceptance of the name "Buffalo Soldiers" by the black troops also supports this explanation.

Fighting Prejudice with Conduct

Personalities and Honors

"Henry Flipper's classic story of refusing to be deterred from success is the essence of the American dream and continues to inspire today."

—Lt. Gen. Larry Jordan, Inspector General, U. S. Army, 1999

The Buffalo Soldiers faced a difficult task on the Texas frontier. Serving alongside white men wearing the same uniforms, the color of their skin prevented them from being accepted as social and political equals. Three black officers were ultimately posted to the Buffalo Soldier regiments. While they were West Point graduates, they were not treated as the officers and gentlemen that their position warranted. Despite the trials and tribulations of the early years, black officers gradually proved their worth and came to be embraced as effective comrades in arms. Early critics claimed that the Buffalo Soldiers would be failures as fighting men. They performed admirably in Texas, fulfilling their duties with dignity and courage.

Over time, they proved their mettle as fighting men, though true equality would be a long time coming. All regiments of the Buffalo Soldiers saw action against the western tribes. Black soldiers distinguished themselves in other ways as well. In 1868, the desertion rate in the U. S. Army was 25%. Desertions in white regiments were three times higher than those in the black regiments and remained significantly higher throughout the Indian war period. Both African American infantry and cavalry regiments had lower rates of alcoholism than did the white regiments.

Henry O. Flipper (1856–1940)

Posted to the Tenth Cavalry Regiment after graduating from West Point in 1877, Flipper hoped to live out his dream of being a lieutenant in the U. S. Army. A promising military career that began at Fort Concho was called into question in his subsequent posting to Fort Davis. Flipper was accused of embezzling government funds from the quartermaster department, falsifying records, and "conduct unbecoming an officer and a gentleman." In a court martial wracked with racial prejudice, Flipper was exonerated of embezzling but found guilty on the other counts and summarily dismissed from the service. He was posthumously pardoned of all crimes in 1999 by President Bill Clinton.

The Tools of the Soldier

Uniforms and Equipment

"The cut of the Jacket and Trowsers is generally bad for the reason that they are cut for goose necked and pot bellied men, neither of which should ever be enlisted."

—Brevet Brigadier General I. N. Palmer, 1867

In the decade after the Civil War, the U. S. Army returned to its prewar levels but was faced with a myriad of tasks, the least of which being making a constant show of force to suppress increasingly hostile Indians. To tighten its appropriations belt, the army made use of the vast quantities of Civil War surplus, much of which was of secondary quality, made of inferior grades of cloth and manufactured in sizes much smaller than Army specifications allowed.

Although the buffalo soldiers were U. S. regulars, their second-class status made them the natural repository for lower-grade clothing. By 1872, surplus stores were depleted to the point that new uniforms could be developed. Issued to all regiments, they provided a new, Prussian-inspired uniform appearance that was a considerable departure from the Spartan simplicity of the Civil War. Civil War surplus remained in use long after the war. A report from an 1872 Washington newspaper: "There are rubber blankets enough on hand to supply all prospective demands for 130 years to come; rubber ponchos and artillery jackets for 80 years, and blouses for 20 years."

Desertions in white regiments were three times higher than those in the black regiments and remained significantly higher throughout the Indian war period. Both African American infantry and cavalry regiments had lower rates of alcoholism than did the white regiments.

ROTATOR 9

Trail Drivers and Longhorns

Hide and Horn

Texas Longhorns

"Other states were carved or born; Texas grew from hide and horn."

—Berta Hart Nance, journalist, from her poem, "Cattle"

The Texas Longhorn descended from English livestock mingled with Spanish beeves. They were rugged, multicolored, and armed with an impressive span of horns that allowed them to defend themselves from predators.

Texas Longhorns multiplied rapidly after their introduction and proved to be wild, cunning creatures that could travel long distances. They thrived in the hostile conditions of the Texas frontier. Persons interested in selling their animals at a profit often had to trail, or drive, these beeves hundreds of miles to market.

This practice had not started in Texas. Settlers in the American South had been trailing livestock to market for generations. During the Civil War, untended herds multiplied several times over, creating a vast resource for energetic young men who wanted to come to Texas, set up a homestead, and round up a herd quickly.

Southern Roots of Texas Trail Drives

- In the Old South, many of the cattle drives were conducted on foot by African American slaves expert at working cattle, including many young slaves who became known as "cowboys."
- Southern livestock herding was based on the "open range"—a concept that said livestock should range freely and be rounded up once a year. Fences were for crops, not animals in the Old South. The Texas frontier presented a vast "open range" for cattlemen.

The Men Who Led the Way

Cattle Drive Icons

"The Texas cattle herder is a character, the like of which can be found nowhere else on earth."

—*Topeka* [Kansas] *Commonwealth*, 1871

Oliver Loving and Charles Goodnight epitomized Texas cattle drivers. Although neither was a native Texan, they created their reputations and their fortunes on the Texas cattle trails. Born in Kentucky in 1812, Oliver Loving moved to Texas in 1840, and eventually settled in Palo Pinto County. He started a thousand-acre ranch and regularly drove his cattle to markets as far away as Illinois and Colorado.

Although the Civil War put him near bankruptcy, he still had access to unclaimed Texas cattle, and he joined in partnership with a young Charles Goodnight.

Goodnight (b. 1836) made his way to Texas from his native Illinois and went into cattle ranching by the late 1850s. After serving as a frontier scout during the Civil War, he joined Loving in driving cattle to Fort Sumner in New Mexico. The partners would make their route famous—the Goodnight-Loving Trail.

Interesting facts about Goodnight and Loving:

- Bose Ikard, a newly freed slave from Parker County, was one of the most respected cowboys working for the partners. Goodnight would later say of him: "He was my detective, banker, and everything else . . . I trusted him more than any living man."
- Goodnight and Loving's first drive to New Mexico in 1866 was the first time a cattle outfit used a chuck wagon—a mobile commissary—for feeding the hands.
- On an 1867 drive, Oliver Loving was badly wounded by Comanches. Carried to Fort Sumner, he died of complications from his wound, but not before he made Goodnight promise to bury him in Texas. Goodnight kept his word.

"The procession of countless cattle on their slow march to the north was one of the most interesting and distinctive features of the West."

—Richard Harding Davis, journalist

The Goodnight-Loving saga has endured well into the modern era, capturing the imaginations of generations of Americans. Author Larry McMurtry's Pulitzer-prize winning 1986 novel *Lonesome Dove*, which was made into a television mini-series in 1989, featured characters Gus Macrae and Woodrow Call, who were loosely based on Oliver Loving and Charles Goodnight.

Where They Went

The Cattle Trails

"The procession of countless cattle on their slow march to the north was one of the most interesting and distinctive features of the West."

—Richard Harding Davis, journalist

The first major route for drives in the 1840s and 1850s was the Shawnee Trail, which passed through Austin and Dallas, then through Indian Territory, and terminated in Kansas and Missouri. After the Civil War the cattle industry picked up again in 1866 with the Goodnight-Loving Trail, following much of the old Butterfield Overland Mail route to New Mexico.

The Chisholm Trail came in 1867 when news that the railroad had reached Abilene, Kansas, making it a destination for trail drives. The route went from Austin to Fort Worth, then through Indian Territory due north to Abilene.

In 1871 John Lytle decided to drive a herd to Dodge City, Kansas, with a more western route through the Callahan Divide, then Indian Territory. Soon the Western (or Dodge City) Trail would become the most heavily used cattle route of them all.

Jobs on the Trail

- Trail boss—in charge of all aspects of the drive; earned about $100 a month plus a share of the profits.
- Ramrods—the drive foreman; earned about $75 a month.
- Cooks—in charge of the chuck wagon; moved ahead of the herd each day to set up camp; earned about $75 a month.
- Wranglers—managed the remuda (horse herd); earned about $50 a month.
- Waddies or Cowboys—drove the herd; earned between $25 and $40 a month.

The Four Great Texas Cattle Trails

- **The Shawnee Trail** thrived from the 1840s through the 1850s.
- **The Goodnight-Loving Trail** provided a steady flow of Texas beef to New Mexico and Colorado from 1866 through the 1870s.
- **The Chisholm Trail** surpassed the Shawnee by the late 1860s as the major northerly route.
- **The Western Trail** became the most-traveled route by the end of the 1870s.

Who Were the Trail Drivers?

Two-thirds of the trail hands (waddies or cowboys) were whites, mostly youths aged twelve to eighteen. Trail bosses and ramrods—also usually whites—were often in their twenties. About a third of trail drivers were African Americans, Hispanics, or Indians; mature men usually, who often served as cooks and as horse wranglers. A few adventurous young women rode the trail, frequently disguised as boys.

The Great Roundup

Owning Cattle in Texas

"The trail life as a whole is easy compared to ranch life."

—Cordia Sloan Duke and Joe B. Franz, cattle ranch authors

Having a cattle ranch in Texas meant being able to prove livestock ownership. Branding was the preferred method to accomplish this. The practice came to the Americas with the Spanish, who used pictographs for their brands rather than letters. Each cattle owner designed his own stylized brand, complete with a flourish of pendants and curlicues.

Cattlemen from the American South also brought branding with them into their Texas ranches. Southern brands tended to include initials of the owners.

Ranchers also identified cattle with the wattle or dewlap—a mark made on the animal's jaw or neck by pinching up the skin and cutting it partially off. The remaining flap of skin hung from the animal in a distinctive manner unique to the owner. More common than wattles were earmarks, which involved cutting a distinct notch or design in one or both ears of the steer.

¿Quién Sabes?

When southerners came to Texas and came into contact with cattle branded in the traditional Spanish fashion, they began to refer to Spanish or Mexican brands as "dog irons," or "¿quién sabes?" (Spanish for "who knows?").

Tradition dictated that cattle owners brand their stock on the left hip. There have been many explanations for this practice:

- Cattle tended to mill more to the right than to the left, so a brand on the left hip would be more visible to cowboys at a roundup as the herds turned clockwise away from the riders.
- Most ropers tended to be right-handed and would therefore generally approach the steer from the left side.
- Some old cowboys claimed that since English is read from left to right, the brand needed to go on the left-hand side because it makes sense to read from "head to tail."

Hashknife Ranch

For at least one frontier Texas cattleman, the name of his ranch came from the shape of his brand. John N. Simpson's peculiar brand was shaped like a hash knife, a common kitchen utensil used to chop vegetables. Simpson partnered with J. R. Couts in 1875 to form the Hashknife Ranch on Elm Creek in Taylor County (site of present Abilene). The two established the ranch headquarters in a dugout on the banks of the creek.

"...for those of us who had a liking for adventure, and a desire to see something of the world, a long ride of two or three weeks, practically in the open air...possesses a wonderful charm...."

—H. D. Barrows

Usually nine or more passengers rode three abreast, squeezed together, with baggage on their laps and mail pouches under their feet. They traveled day and night exposed to the elements and fearful of Indians.

ROTATOR 10

Butterfield Overland Mail

Post by Coach

Coast to Coast

"We rode along at a somewhat rapid pace . . . determined that the overland mail should go through . . . on time."

—Waterman L. Ormsby, journalist and passenger

On March 3, 1857, Congress authorized the Postmaster General to establish transcontinental mail service. The purpose was to appease angry Californians who were clamoring for faster contact with the East. In July, John Butterfield of Utica, New York was awarded a lucrative contract for overland postal delivery. For $600,000 a year, plus all passenger and express receipts, Butterfield agreed to transport mail between the East and the West Coast twice a week for six years. On September 16, 1858, Butterfield coaches began crossing Texas on their way from Tipton, Missouri or Memphis, Tennessee to San Francisco, some 2795 miles. Then, in March of 1861, as the country braced for civil war, this southern route was discontinued in favor of a more northerly line. Suddenly Texas was without regular mail service and a steady link to the outside world.

In spite of its distance and dangerous route through Indian country, John Butterfield's Overland Mail Company provided a major communication and transportation service for much of America.

- John Butterfield spent a year and a million dollars establishing the route that would bear his name.
- Before Butterfield's Overland Mail route, letters sent between the East and West coasts had to travel by ship, either around the horn of South America or with a land leg across Panama.

Mail by Trail

Winding Through Texas

"Above all else, passengers and mail must be protected and schedules maintained . . ."

—John Butterfield, proprietor

After winning the Overland Mail contract in 1857, John Butterfield established a route to get the job done. For political and practical reasons, it wound its way through Texas.

During a time of great enmity between the North and South, the Postmaster General favored a southern route. As a Southerner, he was partial to the South and understood its advantages. The climate provided for year round service, and a string of forts across the breadth of Texas offered protection from Indians.

Butterfield's mail line originated at two points, Tipton, Missouri (linked by rail to St. Louis) and Memphis, Tennessee. At Fort Smith, Arkansas the routes merged, then entered Texas near Sherman. Swinging deep across the Comanche-held frontier, the line left the state at El Paso and skirted the Mexican border before reaching the West Coast and terminating in San Francisco.

A Difficult Task

Readying the Route

"Every month new stations will be built . . . and the roads will be much improved."

—Waterman L. Ormsby, journalist and passenger

When John Butterfield agreed to organize and operate the Overland Mail route, he understood that it had to go into service no later than September 1858. Ahead of him were months of frantic and grueling work to get the line cleared, equipped and ready. As soon as the contract was signed and a route selected, Butterfield proceeded to set up relay stations, buy coaches and wagons, obtain horses and mules, and locate warehouses to store provisions. He also hired superintendents, road bosses, drivers, guards, conductors, keepers, blacksmiths, harness makers, hostelers and clerks.

During the year of preparation, Butterfield drove his workers relentlessly. Bridges were built over rivers, rocks removed from trails, wells dug, roads graded, and mountain passes cleared. Finally, on September 16, 1858, the route was ready and the first stages were on their way.

Preparing the Overland Mail route was a major undertaking. Careful planning, hard work and a million dollars were required to make the route serviceable and safe.

- The Overland Mail Company needed at least 800 men, 139 relay stations, 1800 head of stock and 250 stagecoaches to operate.
- Mail and freight charges were $.10 per one-half ounce and each coach could carry about 12,000 letters in addition to nine or more passengers.
- Typically, 9–12 passengers paid $.15 per mile for short trips or $200 to travel the full length of the Overland Mail route. A ticket that cost $200 in 1860 would cost about $4500 today!
- John Butterfield's Overland Mail contract stipulated that every trip had to be completed within 25 days, which he did without fail.

Riding the Route

Actual Accounts

"An unusually heavy mail in the boot, by weighing down the rear, kept those of us who were on the front seat constantly bent forward . . . ."

—Raphael Pumpelly, passenger

Although John Butterfield's coaches had the mail as their first priority, they also accepted paying passengers. A trip across America by stage was an adventure only for brave and hardy souls. The Overland Mail Company offered passengers point-to-point service across the nation in addition to through service from coast to coast. Coaches traveled 24 hours a day with no overnight stops—only hurried intervals at station houses for a change of horses or mules and perhaps a bite to eat. Occasionally travelers were offered simple meals of bread, coffee, cured meat, and sometimes beans.

Despite popular belief, very few women ever rode the Overland Mail coaches. Those who did usually made short trips in Missouri, Arkansas, and in the settled parts of Texas. Some women cooked for passengers and assisted their husbands with the duties of running a stage station. Riding with the Overland Mail was a bone-jarring ordeal. Usually nine or more passengers rode three abreast, squeezed together, with baggage on their laps and mail pouches under their feet. They traveled day and night exposed to the elements and fearful of Indians. For many, it was a miserable experience. A few found joy in the journey.

Passengers Share Their Thoughts . . .

"The fatigue of uninterrupted traveling by day and night in a crowded coach, and in the most uncomfortable positions, was...producing in me a condition bordering on insanity.... ." —Raphael Pumpelly

"...for those of us who had a liking for adventure, and a desire to see something of the world, a long ride of two or three weeks, practically in the open air... possesses a wonderful charm...." —H. D. Barrows

"Had I not just come out over the route, I would be perfectly willing to go back, but I now know what Hell is like. I've just had 24 days of it." —Waterman L. Ormsby

The Passenger's Observations While Traveling Through Texas . . .

"I shall never forget the gorgeous appearance of the clouds: tinged by the setting sun ...changing like a rapid panorama ...fantastic shapes ...chasing one another through the realms of space."

"...the beautiful moonlight lit up the vast prairie, making its sameness appear like the boundless sea and its hills like the rolling waves." —Waterman L. Ormsby

"The fatigue of uninterrupted traveling by day and night in a crowded coach, and in the most uncomfortable positions, was...producing in me a condition bordering on insanity...."

—Raphael Pumpelly

The most basic early solution to this [housing] problem was to build temporary shelters in the ground called dugouts. Perhaps the most difficulty came, however, when the occasional cow stepped onto the camouflaged roof.

ROTATOR 11

Towns and Social Life

Forming Communities

Early Frontier Towns

"We . . . extend a general invitation to all who are desirous of settling in a good, quiet and orderly town to come and cast their lot with us."

—*Fort Griffin Echo*, 1879

For most of the frontier period, West Texas settlers did not live in towns. The vast prairies, covered with bison and the Plains Indians who followed them, made large groupings of settlers impossible.

The first towns bloomed alongside the frontier forts. Soldiers created a ready market for entrepreneurs who set up businesses near the forts. Merchants, saloonkeepers, and other service people flocked to the small fort settlements. Later, the cattle drives brought more people together in towns along the trails.

Often, these communities took on the reputations of "hell towns," full of gambling and other vices. The buffalo slaughter attracted settlers to other sites, creating hide towns—locations from which the buffalo hides could be shipped. By 1880, with the coming of the railroad to the region, more towns emerged, marking the beginning of the end of the frontier era.

Timeline of a Town—Buffalo Gap

1875—buffalo hunters live in dugouts; one merchant store in a dugout.

1876—hide merchants move to town, construct log cabins; resident population around 30.

1877—post office located in one-room frame house; gamblers and gunmen flock to log cabin saloons; resident population around 100.

1878—made the county seat, sheriff elected, town square has frame businesses (general merchandise and blacksmith), two-story hotel, temporary log cabin courthouse, resident population around 400

1879—construction of large, two-story stone courthouse and jail; a dozen lawyers move to the town; resident population around 500.

1880—twenty-five businesses in town (dry goods stores, grocery stores, two banks, two butcher shops, five saloons, an undertaker, a livery stable, a hotel, and several boarding houses); resident population around 1,000.

A Place to Call Home

Frontier Housing

Upon arriving on the Texas frontier, settlers found their most immediate and daunting challenge to be housing. The most basic early solution to this problem was to build temporary shelters in the ground called dugouts. Similarly, picket cabins consisted of upright pickets placed close together into a trench, then covered with mud and clay in the spaces between the pickets.

For a more permanent structure, some settlers opted for the traditional single-pen log cabin. These buildings needed more uniform hewn logs that could be stacked on each other and interlaced at the corners. These cabins were possible only where settlers found a nice stand of cedars or other hardwood trees.

Finally, settlers also used a building material that was in abundance in West Texas—rocks. Rock buildings provided sturdy structures, but took tremendous amounts of labor to build.

Dugout Particulars

The typical dugout consisted of a rectangular pit, five to seven feet deep, eight to ten feet wide, and of variable length. The roof was made from logs and branches laid across the pit. On these they placed saplings, grass, tow sacks, and any other material that could lend strength, and then they covered the whole structure with dirt. One variation of this type of construction was the partial dugout, which settlers carved into the sides of hills.

Problems with Dugouts

The floors were tamped earth, and everything was "dirty." Dugout residents reported the frequent presence of snakes, spiders, and other pests in the ceiling. Perhaps the most difficulty came, however, when the occasional cow stepped onto the camouflaged roof.

Making Neighbors

Social Life on the Frontier

"There were always feasting and dancing at weddings."

—Sallie Reynolds Matthews, frontier settler

Texas frontier settlers lived isolated lives, but still managed to develop social relations with their neighbors. Holidays, weddings, and the birth of a child would create an excuse for a party. Neighboring families brought food to be served "covered-dish" style to one and all. Another popular amusement for frontier settlers was horse racing. This activity drew people from long distances. Of course, the more prevalent social activity was simply "visitin'." Ranch families would often spend a week or two with friends or family at neighboring ranches.

Religion also played a major role in frontier settlement. Usually, people gathered to worship when itinerate clergy traveled through the area. Established churches only came with the building of towns. Although frontier life was tough and isolated, the people who lived there found enjoyment in their social lives.

Components of a Typical Frontier Wedding

Typically, settlers held the ceremony in the mid-afternoon on the front porch of the bride's parents' home, because there were usually too many people to fit inside. The saying of vows was followed by a feast and a dance that lasted usually until dawn. The "in-fair," a reception held at the groom's parents' house, happened the day after the wedding. A few nights after the wedding, friends would gather at the couples' house around midnight to perform the "charivari." Using horns, pots, pans and other noise-making implements, they made as much noise as possible. According to the custom, the couple could only stop the noise by inviting in the troupe and serving refreshments.

For All that Ails You

Frontier Medicine

"Dr. Boynton went to the patients' homes to tend the ill, riding horseback along trails or paths to the small dwellings."

—Tommie Hazelwood Clack, Frontier Taylor County settler

Illnesses and accidents were part of life on the Texas frontier. Settlers generally had to fend for themselves when it came to medical care. By the 1850s the frontier forts became the only established medical centers in the region. Army doctors cared for soldiers and civilians alike.

By the 1860s, settlers also began consuming patent-medicines sold by merchants in the more settled areas. "Daly's Aromatic Valley Whiskey for Medicinal Purposes" and "Old Sachem Bitters and Wigwam Tonic" were just two of the hundreds of brands that came available in the region.

Women played a major role in nursing the sick back to health. Most children were born with the help of midwives. On trail drives, the cook usually served in the role of physician. When towns started to arrive on the frontier, trained physicians came with them, bringing professional medical practices to the region.

A Variety of Dangers

- Diseases found on the frontier—typhoid, small pox, measles, tuberculosis, tonsillitis, influenza, venereal diseases.
- Sources of wounds on the frontier—guns, arrows, knives, barbed wire, rocks, horses, snakes.
- Life-threatening conditions on the frontier—pregnancy, open cuts (gangrene/sepsis), hypothermia, sun stroke, dehydration, being scalped, bullet/arrow wounds.
- Common folk remedies on the frontier—gunpowder and water paste for sores and wounds, bloodletting for fevers; whiskey for respiratory ailments.

Although frontier life was tough and isolated, the people who lived there found enjoyment in their social lives.

"I felt as if I were alone on a vast sea, and wondered where my next harbor was going to be."
—Sophie A. Poe, ranch wife

Before the frontier disappeared altogether, Army women experienced lives that were both primitive and exotic, exciting yet mundane, and safe but deadly.

ROTATOR 12

Frontier Women

Companions in Exile

Army Wives

"The ladies will have to live in tents all winter, and how much they will suffer is sad to contemplate."

—Lt. Clinton W. Lear, Fifth Infantry, 1851

When General Sherman assembled his forces to prepare for his 1866 campaign to crush Indian resistance, he urged army wives to accompany their husbands to the frontier. Many did, and their presence lent an air of gentility to many a Texas frontier post. Before the frontier disappeared altogether, Army women experienced lives that were both primitive and exotic, exciting yet mundane, and safe but deadly. Embracing Victorian propriety, officers' wives did their best with the scant luxuries that existed within the confines of the frontier fort.

Officers' wives raised their families and lived their lives in an environment where the military caste system separated them from the wives of the soldiers their husbands commanded. Nonetheless, all army wives played an important role in providing a civilizing force upon the frontier army.

Army wives were not the only women present with the army. The Army General Regulations specified:

- "Four women will be allowed to each company as washerwomen and will receive one ration per day each."
- "The price of washing soldiers' clothing, by the month, or by the piece, will be determined by the council of administration."
- "Debts due to the laundress by soldiers, for washing, will be paid or collected in the same way as is prescribed for those due the Sutler, with the laundress having the preference."

"Stand" by Their Man

Buffalo Hunter's Wife

"It was wonderful for me to see them kill the buffalo."

—Ella Elgar Bird, buffalo hunter's wife

The majority of buffalo hunters were young, unmarried men; however, some married men ventured onto the buffalo plains, and they brought their wives with them. Life on the buffalo prairies was quite sparse.

With no timber, most hunters built small rock houses or even tipis to live in with their wives. Hunters' wives worked hard in support of their husbands' endeavors. They usually prepared the meals, and helped stake and dry the hides brought back from a day's hunt. Many hunted wild game for variety in their meals. With no access to extra supplies, hunters' wives had to be creative in preparing the meals.

Because hunters feared for their wives' safety, many taught the women how to fire a rifle. As a result, a few women even went on the hunts with their husbands and participated in the killing and skinning of the buffalo.

Buffalo hunters' wives had to use creativity to make the hunting fields like home. Examples from Ella Bird:

- She cooked buffalo steak daily, but she used a variety of ways—with flour, with wild fruit, broiled, or panseared.

- She used a Winchester rifle to hunt wild turkeys for dinner. She practiced using the rifle by shooting prairie dogs, and she could "shoot the heads off many without missing a shot."
- She reported that they ran out of flour for bread. She borrowed a "large box coffee mill," secured it to the ground, and used it to grind corn into meal for bread. When the corn ran out, she ground peas, reporting that this worked just as well.
- She used a butcher knife to shear the "large heavy mop of wool" off of the dead buffalo heads to make a mattress. She performed this task on "two or three hundred" buffalo.

A Lonely Life

The Cowman's Wife

"A great country for men and dogs, but hell on women and horses."

—Old Texas Proverb

Wives of the cattle herders on the frontier lived lonely, isolated lives. The harsh environment of the frontier also blurred the line between traditional male and female roles. Because the men were often tending cattle away from the home, women had to clear land, chop wood, hunt for food, dig wells, fight prairie fires, and plant and harvest crops.

Ranch women also carried out the traditional female roles on the frontier. They were the primary caregivers to children, they cooked and cleaned the house, cabin, or dugout, and they provided domestic support for their men. Women settlers tended to be from the middle class, with some education. As a result, they had a softening influence on the frontier. They also provided for the religious and practical education of the children. On the whole, women's contributions made ranch families self-sufficient.

Firsthand Accounts

"I am lonesome, Oh! very lonesome . . . I actually think that it is almost a sin for a person to live here where they can scarcely ever see anyone, and are always lonesome. We have been living here over a year and there has been one woman to see us, only one." —Susan E. Newcomb, ranch wife

"At the time, the name of Texas, more especially West Texas, was a synonym for lawlessness, desperadoes, and all that was wild and bad. There was also a leaven of good, those rugged self-disciplined pioneers, men and women of foresight and courage, who were willing to brave the dangerous unknown and undergo countless hardships and privations for the sake of widening their horizons and preparing an easier road for their children." —Sallie Reynolds Matthews, ranch wife

"Our children were early in life well versed in the hardships and privations of pioneer life, and learned to depend on their own broad views and patient industry." —Anne Marie Campbell Reynolds, ranch wife

"I felt as if I were alone on a vast sea, and wondered where my next harbor was going to be." —Sophie A. Poe, ranch wife

"We had no luxuries at that time, and while our homes and furniture were crude and rough, we were all like one family, a neighbor was a real friend, and whatever we had we were willing to share with those less fortunate." —Mrs. J. J. Greenwood, ranch wife

A Life of Toil

Plains Indian Wives

"The [Comanche] women are remarkable for their industry. Besides attending to menial duties . . . they perform extraordinary labors in preparing buffalo hides."

—Nelson Lee, captive of the Comanches for three years

Plains Indian women lived hard lives, but contributed greatly to the well-being of their tribes. Their primary duties were to free the men from burdens that might interfere with their abilities to protect and provide for the tribe. Plains Indian women followed the men, carried household goods, tended the children, and cared for the animals. In some tribes, women also skinned and butchered the bison killed by the men. They tanned the hides, and smoked the meat for the entire band.

Plains Indian women had some property rights, including the right to own horses. However, women were considered the property of their fathers or husbands. Some Comanche women could acquire the supernatural medicine power of their shaman husbands, but only with his permission. In the end, Plains Indian women had few rights, but were still integral to the survival of their tribe.

Comanche Women and Marriage

- Comanche men had to give a gift to their brides' family—usually a horse that he had captured in a raid (horses obtained by other means were not considered worthy).
- When a Comanche woman married, her husband was expected to provide meat to her parents for the rest of their lives.
- Often, if a Comanche man took a second or third wife, he chose the sisters of his first wife, so that he would not have to provide meat for more than one set of in-laws.

"I saw a buffalo hunter come to town one day and market his season's kill for $1500. The next morning, he had to borrow money for his breakfast. The gamblers had gotten it all. The ordinary fellow did not have a ghost of a show in those gambling halls. Most all of the games were crooked and if they could not get it one way, they would another."

—Henry Herron, Fort Griffin resident

ROTATOR 13

Law and Lawlessness

Outlaws and Gamblers

Seedy Side of the Frontier

"Men who had committed crimes, and fleeing from the law, often went as far as they could from civilization, and that was the end."

—Emmett Roberts, rancher, commenting on "The Flat" at Fort Griffin

In the 1870s much of the Texas frontier was a place of transition. Towns like Fort Griffin and Buffalo Gap became the gathering places of many people seeking opportunities. There were cowboys and soldiers, buffalo hunters and merchants. But these places also attracted less scrupulous people—rustlers, gamblers, and prostitutes. The most common type of rustler was the experienced cowboy whose herding practices drifted toward the unethical and illegal. They often grew their herds through theft of others' cattle. Justice was usually swift when they were caught—a noose on a tree. In the towns, there was little in the way of law enforcement, so gamblers preyed on cowboys and hunters in saloons. Prostitution also became a major part of each of the young towns. The presence of these elements gave many of the frontier towns the reputation of general lawlessness.

"Cattle Thieves' Doom"

Words scrawled on a placard fastened to the chests of three corpses found lynched in 1869.

"I saw a buffalo hunter come to town one day and market his season's kill for $1500. The next morning, he had to borrow money for his breakfast. The gamblers had gotten it all. The ordinary fellow did not have a ghost of a show in those gambling halls. Most all of the games were crooked and if they could not get it one way, they would another." —Henry Herron, Fort Griffin resident

"I've seen men and women dancing there in the dance halls without a bit of clothing on." —J. W. Woody, Fort Griffin visitor

"Griffin which has long been the roost of a large quantity of 'soiled doves,' can boast a larger flock than any other town on the frontier." —*Dallas Daily Herald*, 1877 editorial about prostitution in the Flat

The Frontier Saloon

Saloons in the frontier towns attracted some of the most shady characters in Texas. Nevertheless, saloon owners competed with each other for business. In Buffalo Gap, one place was called The Alamo Saloon, while its neighboring business hung out a sign saying that they "Keep the Spirits of Our People Up."

The Bee Hive Saloon in the Flat at Fort Griffin gained fame with the sign at its entrance:

"Within this hive we are all alive; Good whiskey makes us funny. If you are dry step in and try; The essence of our honey."

Making the Frontier "Wild"

Opportunists

"Doc Holliday was afraid of nothing on earth."

—William Barclay "Bat" Masterson, buffalo hunter and lawman

The rustlers, gamblers, and prostitutes that brought such a seedy reputation to the Texas frontier were opportunists. They flocked to the region where there was little law enforcement, and ready cash was available for the taking.

Despite the heavy penalty for rustling cattle, numerous men tried to gain their fortunes in this manner because of the sheer number of steers on the plains. Similarly, gamblers knew to come to the frontier because of the vast amounts of easy targets among the hunters and cowboys.

Prostitution also thrived because of the large number of young, unmarried men who made up the majority of the population of the frontier. Many "soiled doves" worked the frontier towns during the era.

Gambling on the Texas Frontier

By far the most popular saloon gambling game was Faro—a fast-paced card game in which money changes hand on every draw. Dice games such as "high/low," "chuck-a-luck," and "grand hazard" were also popular. Poker was not as popular, but a version of five-card draw did appear in the frontier Texas saloons.

A Blurry Boundary

Good Guys or Bad Guys?

"Fast is fine, but accuracy is everything."

—Wyatt Earp

The distinction between law and lawlessness was frequently a blurry one on the Texas frontier. Men who might be considered lawbreakers in one circle worked as law enforcement in others.

In Reconstruction Texas, men on the wrong side of the law were often caught up in disputes over larger political issues often associated with efforts to refight the Civil War. In these instances, they tried to use the thinly-veiled guise of "the law" to settle personal scores, best typified by the Sutton-Taylor Feud which consumed West Texas in the mid 1870s.

These conflicts were every bit as passionate as those which had divided the nation, and further blurred the lines between right and wrong. In many cases, those who fought for, and against, the law lived and died at the end of a gun.

Firsthand Accounts

"A killing was one of the ordinary, expected events of the night, on which comments were over and the incident closed by the time the blood had been mopped up from the floor." —R. A. Slack, Fort Griffin resident

"Hang 'em first, then if they persist in their innocent amusement, cremate them." —George W. Robson, editor, *Fort Griffin Echo*, on habitual criminals

"Bad meat draws flies; Leave or you are doomed." —Vigilante notice to outlaws, Fort Griffin

"I believe that if a man was to shoot me through the heart I would kill that man before I died." —John Larn, lawman and suspected cattle rustler

"On the morning of the 24 ult., Mr. Louis Collins was killed by some unknown parties in the back room of the Alamo Saloon. The deceased was a cow-boy." —The first edition of the *Buffalo Gap News*, 1879

Cornerstone of Civilization

The Rule of Law

"At night a party of armed men went to the jail and shot Larn to death."

—*Frontier Echo* article, 1878

By the late 1870s, as more settlers moved into the Texas frontier, lawlessness began to be challenged. Americans had been steeped in the traditions of the rule of law, and they saw a need for order in their frontier towns.

At first without any strong law enforcement presence, some citizens took the law into their own hands. Vigilante groups formed and dispensed justice as they saw fit. State and federal law enforcement in the form of Texas Rangers and Federal Marshals came next.

It was the local drive for law, however, that would have the most lasting effects. Citizens established county seats and elected sheriffs from among their neighbors. Then they set to work building courthouses as the first major public buildings. These temples of justice helped to turn the tide. The era of the wild frontier was coming to an end.

"I believe that if a man was to shoot me through the heart I would kill that man before I died."

—John Larn, lawman and suspected cattle rustler

The demise of the buffalo changed the landscape, and made huge tracts of land available for agricultural use.

Railroads defined where future towns in West Texas would be established.

ROTATOR 14

End of an Era

An Industrial Nation

Technology Conquers the Frontier

"Light as air, stronger than whiskey, and cheap as dirt."

—John Warne Gates, on barbed wire

The Texas frontier was also changing. While working conditions for the early settlers had been arduous, job security was almost nonexistent. New technology in the form of the six-shot revolver and the high-powered rifle had led to removal of the Indians and the near extinction of the buffalo.

The demise of the buffalo changed the landscape, and made huge tracts of land available for agricultural use. However, use of this land also came to be dependent upon the use of new technology.

As big business grew, its products soon became available to all Americans, regardless of how isolated they thought they were. By 1880, barbed wire began to divide the prairie, closing the open range. The addition of windmills solved many of the water worries of frontier Texans, opening up the region to commercial crop planting.

Barbed wire forever changed the look and feel of West Texas. Its sales steadily increased from the time of its introduction:

- Amount of barbed wire sold in 1876—3 million pounds
- Amount of barbed wire sold in 1879—80 million pounds

The Machine on the Prairie

The Railroad Arrives

"In building the Texas and Pacific we . . . want a road through Texas which the country, when settled, is capable of supporting by its local trade when built."

—General Grenville M. Dodge, 1880

In 1871, the Texas and Pacific Railroad was chartered to build westward towards Yuma, Arizona. Although plans were in place to link the railroad with the Southern Pacific, by 1877, the T&P was bankrupt. With lines extending no further west than Fort Worth, stockholders in the Southern Pacific realized that their line would be worthless without an eastern terminus, and pressured Congress for the rights to the T&P land grants. Circumventing Congress, the Arizona and New Mexico territorial governments obtained charters to allow the Southern Pacific to build eastward.

In 1879, T&P President Thomas Scott, secured investments from Jay Gould, George Pullman, and others to fund construction on the T&P. Beginning in January 1880, Gould and Russell Sage took over as directors of the T&P and began extending the railroad and telegraph lines westward.

The Texas and Pacific Railroad

The T&P was originally chartered by the U.S. government for military purposes. Its charter stated that its purpose was to insure the carrying of the mails, troops, munitions of war, supplies and stores of the United

States. When chartered, the T&P was charged with opening 100 miles of track in the first two years, then 100 miles per year thereafter, and to provide a link to the Pacific coast within ten years.

Following the Rails

The Impact of the Railroad

"We are no prophets . . but the opinion prevails that we will get the T. & P. [Railroad] here . . . . There are few towns this side of New York City that do not believe it."

—*Buffalo Gap News*, 1880 [six months before the T&P announced it was bypassing Buffalo Gap]

Railroads defined where future towns in West Texas would be established. Arriving in Baird in 1880, the T&P soon began praising the advantages of West Texas

When the railroad bypassed his home in Belle Plain, Colonel Claiborne Merchant tried buying land in Buffalo Gap, anticipating the future route of the T&P. When he found no property for sale, he looked elsewhere, purchasing in northern Taylor county. In conjunction with Hashknife Ranch owner John N. Simpson and others, Merchant entered into an agreement with the T&P. He gave the company the land needed for a depot, track siding, and cattle pens at a much reduced price, and the company would lay out a new town, promote it, and stage an auction for town lots. After Abilene was created, Sweetwater and Colorado City sprang up along the T&P's route, leaving other communities to wither away.

Under the direction of railroad magnate Jay Gould, and using construction techniques created by Morgan Jones, the Texas and Pacific Railroad built 994 miles of line across Texas in 1881. Many called Jay Gould a "robber baron." He became known for buying rundown railroads, making cosmetic improvements, using company capital to pay dividends to stockholders, then selling out with a profit.

Gray's Railroad map of Texas, 1877–8.

A buffalo hide tipi is reconstructed in Frontier Texas! A tipi often required up to twenty skins.

CHAPTER 10

The Making of Frontier Texas!

First a bone yard, then junk pile, and now a cultural gem.

A new facility for downtown was designed to reflect the region's past and inspire visitors and future generations.

An 1883 Sanborn Insurance map of Abilene shows livestock pens and a loading ramp on the location where Frontier Texas! sits today. Although the buffalo hide industry had passed its peak years earlier, bones were scattered throughout the region. This created a great economic opportunity and a business was soon established on this location named Texas Hide and Bone. People from all over the region brought buffalo bones to be sold.

After all of the buffalo bones had been collected and sold, the business moved into scrap metal. In 1905 the business name

DRAWN BY AUGUSTUS KOCH.
1. M. E. Church.
2. School House.
3. Hotel and Passenger Depot of the Texas and Pacific R. R.
BIRDS EYE VIEW OF
ABILENE
TAYLOR COUNTY, TEXAS. 1883.
5. Wm. Ca eron's Lumber Yard.
NORTH SEVENTH STREET
NORTH SIXTH STREET
NORTH FIFTH STREET
NORTH FOURTH STREET
NORTH THIRD STREET
NORTH SECOND STREET
SOUTH FIRST STREET
SOUTH SECOND STREET
SOUTH THIRD STREET
SOUTH FOURTH STREET
SOUTH FIFTH STREET
SOUTH SIXTH STREET
SOUTH SEVENTH STREET
MULBERRY
PEACH
PALM
POPLAR
BUTTERNUT
ELM
SYCAMORE
OAK
PECAN
LOCUST
CEDAR
CYPRESS
PINE
WALNUT
MESQUITE
PLUM
CHINA

changed to Texas Hide and Metal. That business remained in this location until the City of Abilene purchased the property in the 1990s. The scrap metal business relocated two miles north and was renamed Texas Metals & Recycling Company.

Facility Concept

In 1999 the Texas Department of Transportation announced a federal plan, the T-21 Reimbursement Program, and indicated that proposed visitor center facilities would be viewed with favor in the allocation of those funds. Volunteers in Abilene began developing a concept that might gain T-21 seed money while providing a productive use for a site downtown that had been occupied for decades by a railroad storage yard and a commercial recycling center—seven acres that the City of Abilene had recently acquired.

The stimulation of downtown Abilene was the core motivation in this project. An entity was needed that could increase downtown activity by attracting local residents and their guests as well as regional visitors and tourists—and in doing so might become an economic engine for other attractions and businesses in Abilene as well. The concept of a visitor center coupled with an attraction emerged to fulfill this need to increase downtown activity. In addition, the facility helped to provide exposure for Abilene and the newly resuscitated Texas Forts Trail as the communities of the region promote themselves to potential visitors.

The attraction portion of the project evolved into a historical experience, a walk-through that would capitalize on the rich—though often unrecognized—history of the region featuring the real people who were involved in transforming this wilderness into our current definition of civilization.

Facility Purpose

In the same way that Texas' early frontier forts established a protective gateway at the edge of western civilization, Frontier Texas! established itself as a welcoming gateway at the limits of downtown Abilene. An important component of the continuing revitalization of the downtown area, the project functions both as the "trailhead" for Abilene and the Texas Forts Trail and as a destination in itself. One wing of the building is a Visitors Center for the City of Abilene, for the "Big Country" region of west Texas, and for the Texas Forts Trail, a 700-mile heritage tourism loop which starts and ends in Abilene. The larger part of the building is an audio-visual and interactive center. The original exhibit, opened in 2004, titled "The Century of Adventure" featuring cowboys and longhorns, soldiers and forts, Indians, the buffalo trade, and vignettes of frontier life from 1780–1880. A new exhibit, opened in 2013, titled "Blood & Treasure on the Frontier" expanded the time period to include prehistoric Texas, added new characters, new artifacts a series of murals, and a Guns of the West display.

The site on which Frontier Texas! was built.

Architectural Design

The architecture firm Good, Fulton & Ferrell of Dallas designed the Frontier Texas! building and won an award from the American Institute of Architects for outstanding design on the project. The Tittle Luther Partnership managed the project.

Since Frontier Texas! is a facility intended to welcome, entertain and educate, the design of the building and site was approached with the idea that architecture should further these objectives. Extensive research into the organization and architecture of the original frontier forts formed the basis for many of the major design decisions. At the same time, the City of Abilene desired to create a memorable image based upon that history. The Frontier Texas! building was designed to present a lesson in itself.

The design of the facility contrasts heavy masonry and metal roofs with open running porches supported by slender columns. The two components are reflected differently in the architecture: the exhibit wing and other "storytelling" building elements are constructed of rough local limestone with minimal openings, detailed and proportioned to suggest the load bearing wall construction of the frontier forts. The Visitors Center portion is treated in a more modern way. Its structural frame is expressed, clad in large masonry units, and large areas of glass fill the spaces between the columns. The building elements form the edges of a large open area scaled to recall the parade grounds around which the frontier forts were organized.

The site is located on the eastern edge of downtown Abilene, at the intersection of a major north/south thoroughfare and the primary east/west connection between I-20 and downtown. As such, the building is the first face of downtown that one encounters entering downtown from the interstate. An active Union Pacific railroad line forms the southern edge of the site. Planning for the site incorporated a new street connection, providing more direct access from the Interstate directly to the downtown area.

The organization of the site was based on the organization of the forts themselves. Figure "A" below shows the plan of Fort Davis. Like all of the forts from this era, the component buildings are organized around a central rectangular parade ground, with a large flagpole at the center. Figure "B" below is a conceptual sketch of the site organization at Frontier Texas! illustrating how this historic strategy was applied to the modern building. The large portion of the building running east/west houses the exhibit component of the facility, and the smaller portion which divides the site from north to south represents the Visitors Center. These volumes and a rubble wall sheltered by a trellis define the parade ground. The Visitors Center is used to mark a "temporal datum", separating the front of the site which addresses downtown in a modern way, from the more historically referential back of the site.

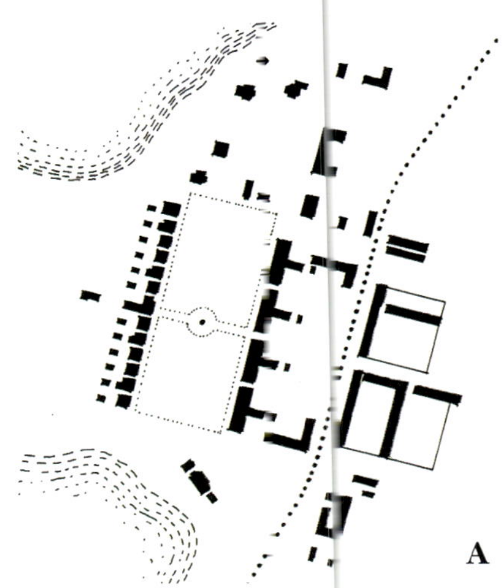

A

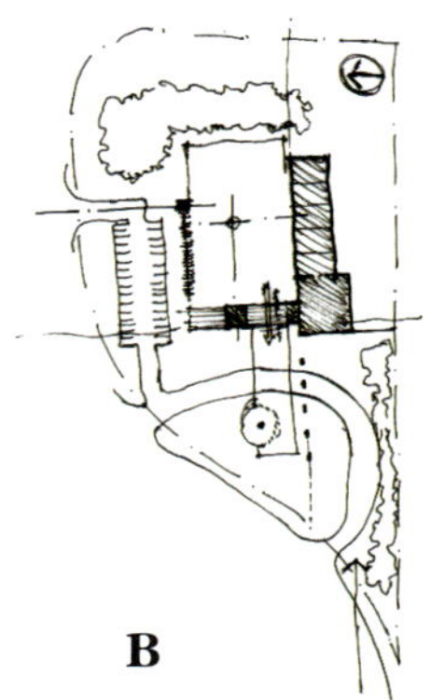

B

Historic Architectural Elements

The buildings at Frontier Texas! are intended to recall, but not mimic, the architecture of the frontier forts. The original forts were built by the soldiers that were stationed there. As such, the materials they used were mostly local, and the construction techniques were simple and straightforward. Building orientation and proportions were designed to take advantage of prevailing breezes, and to provide shelter from the Texas sun. Covered walkways and porches were common as a means to provide shelter from the elements. The most important buildings, such as the armory and Commandant's office, were placed on axis with the parade ground. The enlisted quarters and mess halls occupied one of the long sides of the parade ground, with officers' quarters on the opposite side. All of these have in some way served as inspiration for the design of Frontier Texas!

LEFT: Ft. Belknap, near Graham, Texas.
RIGHT: View of the Exhibit Wing, Frontier Texas!

The natural limestone used on the majority of the exterior of Frontier Texas! was quarried less than 40 miles from the site.

LEFT: Officer's Quarters from Parade Ground, Ft. Concho, San Angelo, Texas.
RIGHT: View of the Visitors Center from Parade Ground.

The Visitors Center is positioned as would be any important structure on a frontier fort. It serves as the main public access building at Frontier Texas! The transparent façade is intended to allow the Parade Ground to be viewed from the front of the building upon arrival.

LEFT: Ft. Concho, San Angelo, Texas.
RIGHT: View of North Canopy, Frontier Texas!

A modern interpretation of the wood framed porches and canopies of the forts, the covered walks at Frontier Texas! are framed in steel for durability, with wood decks and metal roofs used to recall the original methods of construction. As they do at the original forts, these porches link the entire facility.

LEFT: Parade Ground, Ft. Griffin, near Albany, Texas.
RIGHT: View of Flagpole, Frontier Texas!

Navy surplus main masts from decommissioned warships were often used as the flagpoles at the frontier forts. The 60' tall flagpole at Frontier Texas! was specially fabricated for this project. Its stepped main mast, gaff, and yard arms can display up to four flags simultaneously.

Today, the state of the remaining frontier forts varies from substantially restored to varying stages of ruin. In its capacity as the "trailhead" for the Texas Forts Trail, another design goal for Frontier Texas! was to take inspiration from these ruins, and to provide the visitor with a glimpse of what these sites will look like when they arrive.

LEFT: Powder Magazine, Ft. Belknap, near Graham, Texas
RIGHT: Powder Magazine, Frontier Texas!

The "powder magazine" at Frontier Texas! is used as an organizational element of the site, providing a terminus for the arbor along the northern edge of the parade ground, and marking the axis of Ash Street north of the site.

LEFT: Chimney remnants, Fort Phantom Hill, Abilene, Texas
RIGHT: Entry Pylons, Frontier Texas!

All that remains of Fort Phantom Hill outside of Abilene are its dramatic masonry chimneys. The stone pylons at the Frontier Texas! entrance plaza are a response to these elements, and provide an extension of the parade ground's southern edge through the facility's entry plaza. These slender forms provide a backdrop for a monumental bronze buffalo, symbolic of the importance of the buffalo during the frontier era, both as a source of food and clothing for the Native Americans and of the buffalo hunts as an economic engine during the westward expansion of white culture.

The People Behind the Scenes

It took a talented group of people to imagine and create this great facility. Each played their own role in stitching together the stories, imagining and designing displays, editing stories and films, painting pictures and building sets that can withstand thousands of hands reaching out to touch the past.

- **H. C. Zachry**—Even if he doesn't like the title, he is the visionary founder of Frontier Texas!, because without his countless volunteer hours the facility would not exist.
- **The Historians**—Dr. Don Frazier, Dr. Daniel Gelo, Bob Green and Bruce Shackelford.
- **Pyramid Studios, Richmond, Virginia**—Bruce and Dixie Hornstein played a key role in designing and producing the audio-visual elements that tell the stories in a beautiful, dramatic way.
- **Exhibit Concepts, Dayton, Ohio**—The exhibit fabrication team that built the sets, put the artistic touches on almost every surface of the exhibits and built everything to last for a generation of use from excited school children.

The 2013 Redevelopment Team

In early 2012 the museum undertook a major redevelopment of the exhibits that opened on March 2, 2013. The local committee included H. C. Zachry, Kim Snyder (Board President), Jeff Salmon (Executive Director), Scott Clowdus (Operations Director), Pam Thomas (Museum Educator) and historian Don Frazier. Pyramid Studios of Richmond, Virginia was hired to lead the redesign. Brent Johnson Design of Boston, Massachusetts provided exhibit design and Exhibit Concepts of Dayton, Ohio once again provided fabrication. Harris Acoustics of Abilene built the completely new welcome theater.